73
COOL
SCIENCE
TRICKS

to Wow Your Friends!

ANNA CLAYBOURNE

ARCTURUS

ARCTURUS

This edition published in 2021 by Arcturus Publishing Limited
26/27 Bickels Yard, 151–153 Bermondsey Street,
London SE1 3HA

Author: Anna Claybourne
Illustrator: Josephine Wolff
Editor: Stephanie Carey and Cloud King Creative
Designer: Nathan Balsom
Design Manager: Jessica Holliland
Editorial Manager: Joe Harris

ISBN: 978-1-83940-616-4
CH007353NT
Supplier 29, Date 1220, Print run 10183

Printed in China

What is STEM?

STEM is a world-wide initiative that
aims to cultivate an interest in
Science, Technology, Engineering, and
Mathematics, in an effort to promote
these disciplines to as wide a variety
of students as possible.

CONTENTS

INTRODUCTION

Want to amaze your friends and family with mindboggling tricks, games, and experiments? You've come to the right place!

What is science?

Science just means "knowledge." It's about understanding how everything in the world works, what it's made of, and how we can use it.

To find out about all this stuff, scientists do tests and experiments. They observe what happens when they mix things together, heat things up, or cool them down. They experiment with different materials, and things like electricity, floating, melting and freezing, and magnets.

For example, when early people learned how to make fire, and use it for cooking, that was science!

Arabic scientist Hasan Ibn al-Haytham figured out how light travels in straight lines to our eyes, and can make an upside-down image inside a dark room (see page 69!)

Isaac Newton realized how objects are pulled toward the Earth by the force of gravity ...

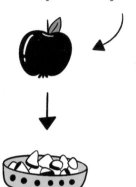

... and Agnes Pockels did experiments to understand surface tension on the surface of water (see page 17).

What just happened?

Sometimes, the results of science experiments seem weird, unexpected, or amazing!

Everyday things like air, water, forks, eggs, and even our own brains can work in some pretty strange ways ... as you'll discover in this book. But it's not magic—it's science!

With a little sneaky science knowledge, you can blow your friends' minds in all kinds of ways! Make things disappear, defy gravity, conjure up confusing illusions, and make amazing artistic and musical creations, edible experiments, and cool light and sound effects. Read on to find out how!

RAISIN' THE RAISIN!

You know how some things float, and some things sink?
Well, a plain old raisin can do both!

The trick

Pour recently opened sparkling water or lemonade into a clear glass. Now drop a raisin into your drink so that it sinks to the bottom, and then watch and wait. Nothing happening? Give it a minute or two. Eventually, you should see the raisin start to float up to the surface.

But wait! After a while at the surface, the raisin will go back down again. And then up again. And on and on, rising and sinking like a tiny, wrinkly submarine. Try adding more raisins for an up-and-down raisin disco.

What's going on?

Raisins are denser (heavier for their size) than plain water, so they sink. However, sparkling drinks contain dissolved carbon dioxide gas. The bubbles appear as gas is released from the liquid. As the raisin sits at the bottom of the glass, some of the bubbles stick to its rough surface. Eventually, there are enough gas bubbles on the raisin to make it float. But when the raisin reaches the surface, the gas bubbles pop and escape into the air. Now the raisin is heavier again, so down it goes. By collecting and then losing gas bubbles, the raisin changes its overall density, so it floats and then sinks.

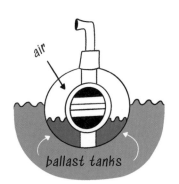
air

ballast tanks

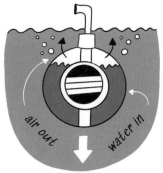
air out

water in

water out

air in

Did you know?

Have you ever wondered how a submarine sinks and rises? It's actually similar to the rising raisin. Submarines have spaces in them called ballast tanks. To make the sub sink, the ballast tanks are filled with seawater. To make it float, compressed air is released, pushing the water out. Like the bubbles on the raisin, this makes the sub less dense overall, and it floats back up.

BRIDGE THE GAP!

As we all know, a bridge has to be pretty strong. That's why they're made of paper.
Wait a minute, no they're not! But for this trick, paper is all you've got. Can you do it?

the trick

All you need is a piece of paper, and three full, unopened drink cans. The challenge is to make a bridge between two of the cans, using the paper. Oh, and it has to be strong enough to hold up the third can!

Challenge your friends or family to make a strong enough bridge, and they'll be totally stumped! But here's the secret—lay the paper on a flat surface, and fold over the ends, first one way, and then the other, in a zigzag pattern.

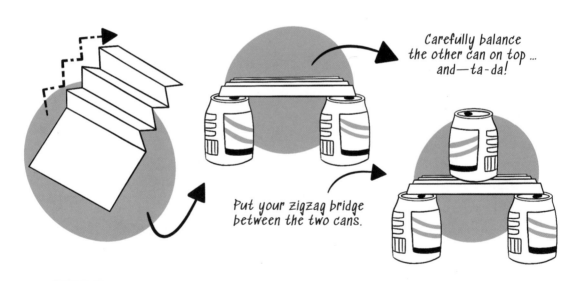

Carefully balance the other can on top ... and—ta-da!

Put your zigzag bridge between the two cans.

What's going on?

A flat piece of paper makes a useless bridge, because as soon as you put a weight on it, it bends. But when you fold it, you change the shape so that the weight presses on the edges of the paper folds. Each fold makes a triangle shape—one of the strongest, most stable shapes to build with.

Did you know?

Triangles are exceptionally strong because they don't collapse easily.

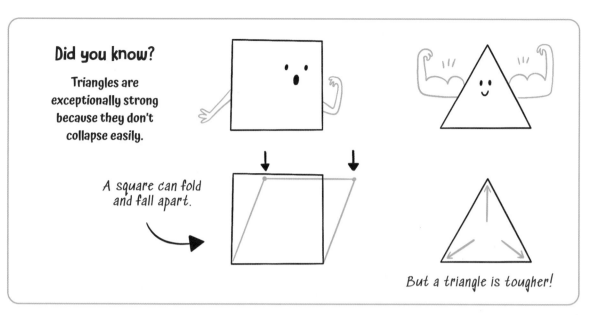

A square can fold and fall apart.

But a triangle is tougher!

For this reason, architects sometimes use triangle shapes for earthquake-proof buildings, like the Transamerica Pyramid in San Francisco, USA.

THE IMPOSSIBLE FORKS

This trick looks totally impossible—until you see it right there in front of you! Guaranteed to blow your friends' minds.

the trick

Find a glass, and a matchstick or toothpick. Can you make the stick balance with one end on the edge of the glass, and the other end sticking out—like this?

Impossible, huh? But it can be done. You just need to make the stick heavier, by hanging some forks on it. Yes, you read that correctly.

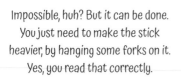

 The fork handles add weight here:

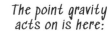 The point gravity acts on is here:

Take two metal forks and fit them onto the end of the stick, like this. It will take a bit of adjusting, but once you get it right, the stick will balance on its end.

What's going on?

How can the stick balance on one end?
It's all down to some super-simple science. An object balances on its center of gravity. But the center of gravity isn't always in the middle. It's just the point that has the weight evenly spread out around it.

In the impossible forks trick, the forks and the match together make an unusual shape.

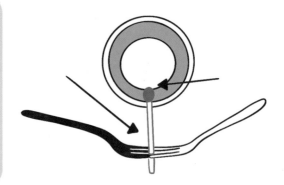

Why not try?

If you love the impossible
forks, try the coin version, too!
Slot the forks onto one edge of
a coin, and try to balance the coin
on the opposite edge.

11

HOW STRONG IS AN EGG?

Eggshells are delicate and easy to break, right?
Well, only sometimes! Prepare to be amazed ...

the trick

For this trick, you'll need four eggs, and an adult to help. Break the eggs neatly in half, and empty them out (save them to make something tasty later). Carefully wash out the eggshells with warm water and soap. Then place the pointy upper halves on a towel on the floor, like this:

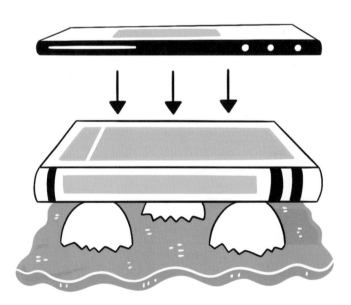

Next, lay a large hardback book on top of the eggshells. How many more books do you think you can add to the pile before they crack under the pressure?

What's going on?

You'll probably find it's a LOT more books than you guessed. If you know someone quite small, they may even be able to STAND on the bottom book without the shells cracking! Although eggshell is thin and breakable, the shape of an egg gives it its strength. When you press down on the top, the forces are directed down through the sides, making it hard to break.

Did you know?

The strong shape of eggs helps to stop them breaking when a bird sits on them in the nest, until the baby inside is ready to peck its way out. Pecking breaks the shell, just like when you tap an egg on the side of a bowl.

THE INCREDIBLE EGG DROP

No one will believe you can make the egg fall into the glass
of water without touching or breaking it ... but you can!

the trick

First, set up the trick. You'll need a fresh egg, and a glass big
enough for it to fall into. Half-fill the glass with water, and
stand it on a tray. On top of the glass, put a plastic or metal
picnic plate. Find a cardboard toilet-paper tube, and stand it
in the middle. Then, on top of that, place the egg on its side.
You're ready!

To make the egg fall into the glass, simply
whack the plate with a fast, sideways movement,
as shown below. The egg will fall straight down
and drop into the water.*

Splash!

*At least, that's what should happen! Before demonstrating this trick, you may
want to test it out first. The tray will catch the mess, if it goes wrong.

What's going on?

The egg drop works because of a force called inertia. Inertia makes an object keep doing what it's doing—whether it's moving, or staying still. The egg is still, and stays that way, unless another force makes it move.

When you hit the plate, the plate and the tube fly out of the way so quickly that the tube doesn't have a chance to move the egg. The egg is suspended in mid-air until gravity pulls it straight down—and ... PLOP!

PING-PONG PUZZLER

You may think that if you blast a ping-pong ball with a hairdryer,
it would simply fly away across the room ... think again!

The trick

All you need is a ping-pong ball, and a hairdryer (ask to
use it first!) Switch on the hairdryer, and point it upward.
Then hold the ping-pong ball in the flow of air, and let go.
As if by MAGIC, it stays there!

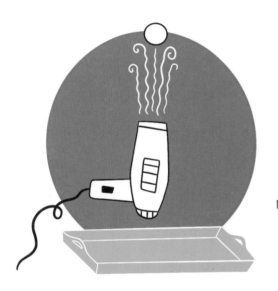

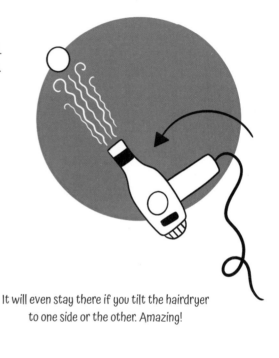

It will even stay there if you tilt the hairdryer
to one side or the other. Amazing!

What's going on?

**The ball stays up because the stream of
air is pushing it up—but why doesn't it get
blown off sideways?** As the air hits the ball,
it flows closely around it, thanks to an effect
called the "Coandă effect."
This creates low pressure, which pulls the ball
sideways. But because it's being pulled on
all sides, it stays in the middle.

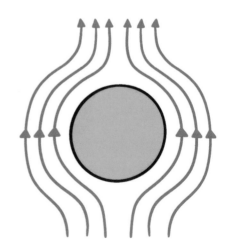

SOAPY SPEEDBOAT

To make a speedboat that zooms across the water,
you don't need paddles, propellers, or sails—just soap!

the trick

Cut out a small cardboard boat shape (copy the shape below) from a piece of flat craft foam. (If you don't have any craft foam, a cereal box will do.) Pour some water into a plastic tray or plate, and place the boat at one side.

Put a bit of liquid soap on your finger, and dab it onto the sides of the notch at the back of the boat. Then watch it go!

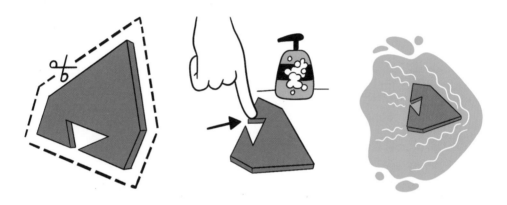

What's going on?

A force called surface tension makes the molecules on the surface of the water pull toward each other. When you add the soap, it reduces the surface tension behind the boat. But in front of the boat, it's still strong. The water molecules there pull together, and pull the boat with them. Agnes Pockels first noticed this effect when she was washing the dishes, so she did some experiments and then wrote the first paper on surface tension.

DEFY GRAVITY!

Not one, not two, but THREE ways to turn a cup of water upside down, without any spilling out!

the trick 1: Water whirl

This works best with a paper cup. Cut a piece of string about 1 m (3 feet) long. Make small holes in the sides of the cup, feed through each end, and tie with knots.

Fill the cup 2/3 full with water. Then holding the string, carefully swing the cup to and fro, then up and around in a full circle.

(Do this outdoors to be safe!)

What's going on?

The force holding the water in is known as centpetal force. As you twirl the cup, you move the water, and it tries to fly away in a straight line. But the string and the cup hold it back, so it ends up staying in the cup. It only works if you whirl it fast enough!

the trick 2:
Postcard trick

For this one, use a plastic cup. Fill it right up to the brim with water. Then lay a postcard on top. Holding the postcard with your hand, flip the cup completely upside down ... then let go! What happens? Nothing!

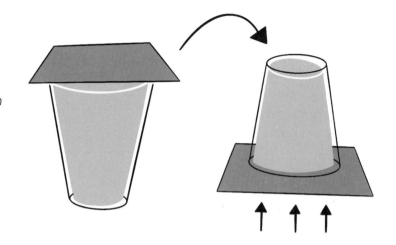

What's going on?

The air all around us pushes on objects from all sides, with a force called air pressure. The air pressure pushing upward on the postcard is stronger than the gravity pulling the water down—so it stays in!

the trick 3:
Magic mesh

One more trick to try! This time, fill the cup to the brim, then stretch a fine cloth, such as a T-shirt or handkerchief, tightly over the top. Holding the cloth in place quickly flip the cup upside down.

Look! No spills!

What's going on?

The cloth is full of small holes. But when it's pulled tight, surface tension creates a force that holds the water together so it doesn't escape.

STRAW OF STEEL

Can your friends solve this potatoey puzzle? Simply ask them to take a paper drinking straw, and stick it through a raw potato.

The trick

They'll probably have a LOT of trouble with the straw bending and folding when they try to stick it in the potato. But there is a secret—to make it work, hold the straw with your thumb over the top end, as shown below. Then stab the straw hard into the potato, and ... Voilà!

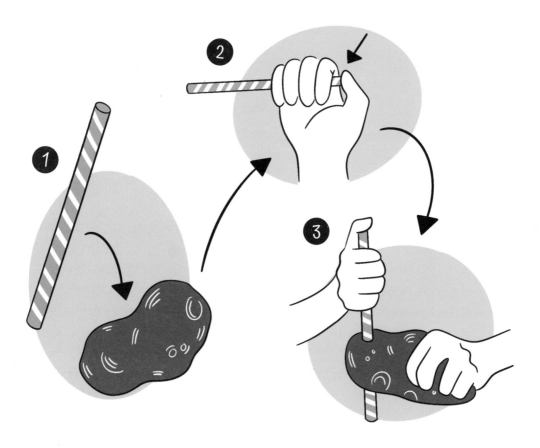

What's going on?

When you put your thumb over the end, you trap air inside the straw, making it stiffer and stronger (a bit like inflating a long, thin balloon). The more the straw pushes into the potato, the more the air inside gets squeezed, making the straw stronger.

DOUBLE BOUNCE

If you drop a bouncy ball, it will never bounce back to the same height from which it started. Unless you know the special trick, that is!

the trick

First, try dropping a ball to see how high it bounces. Whether it's a rubber ball, tennis ball, or soccer ball, it can't bounce back as high. That's because some of its energy is used up when it hits the ground, and makes a sound.

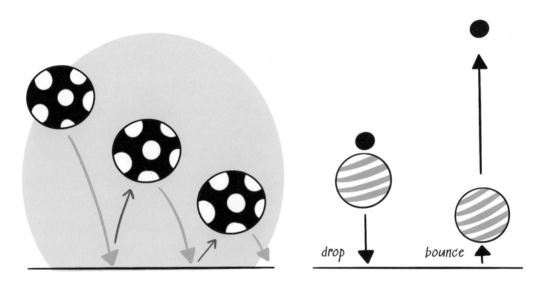

drop   bounce

Now for the trick! Take a large bouncy ball, such as a soccer ball, and hold a smaller ball on top of it. Let them go at the same time. BOINNGGG! The smaller ball bounces incredibly high!

What's going on?

When the two balls land, the small one lands on top of the big one, which acts like a trampoline. As the big ball bounces back up, its pushing power passes into the smaller ball giving it extra energy, and an extra-high bounce!

PAPER POWER

Prepare to experience the power of paper! All you need is a large sheet of newspaper or wrapping paper, and a wooden ruler.

the trick

Place the ruler on a table, with almost half of it sticking out over the edge. Then spread the sheet of paper over the top, lined up with the edge of the table. Smooth it down as flat as you can, and press it down gently around the ruler.

Now, all you have to do is lift up the paper, by hitting down on the other end of the ruler as hard as you can. Go!

What do you mean, it didn't work?

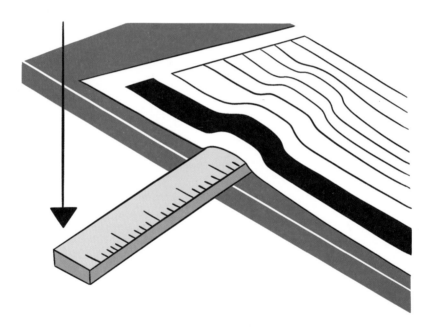

What's going on?

The thin sheet of paper can somehow hold down the ruler—but how? The truth is, it's not actually the paper that has the power—it's the air. The bigger the area of the paper, the more air pressure there is pressing down on it. If it's a big sheet of paper, there's enough air pressure to hold the ruler in place.

If you press the ruler down more gently, though, you'll succeed. That's because this allows time for air to be sucked in under the paper. Then the air pressure is equal above and below the paper, so it lifts up easily.

Did you know?

The air pressure all around us comes from the atmosphere—the blanket of air all around the Earth. Most of this air is in a layer about 100 km (about 60 miles) thick.

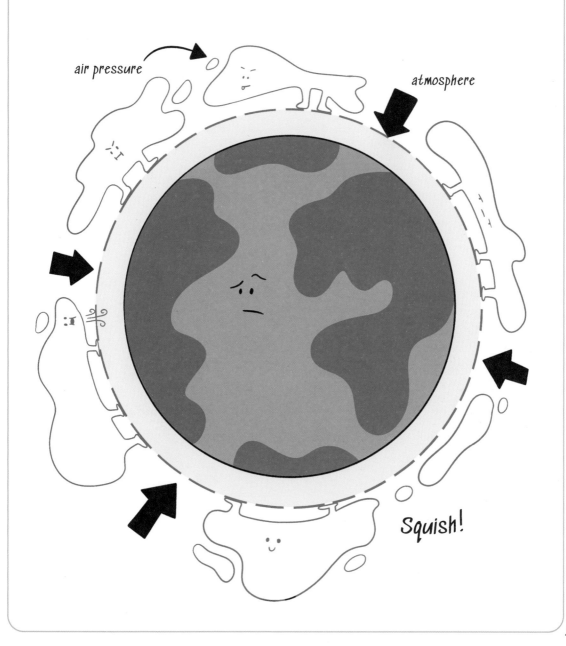

air pressure

atmosphere

Squish!

BOTTLE-BLOW CHALLENGE

What could be easier than blowing a ball into a bottle?
In fact, it's harder than it looks!

the trick

First, you'll need a large plastic bottle that's clean and empty. Then roll up a piece of paper into a small, tight ball. It should be small enough to fit into the neck of the bottle easily, without getting stuck.

Lay the bottle on its side, and place the paper ball into the opening. Now challenge your friends to blow the ball inside the bottle. Easy, right? But when they try it, the ball will just shoot back out!

Try it with other objects, too, like a small toy or a mini pom-pom.

What's going on?

The problem is, the bottle is already full. Full of air, that is!
When you drop an object into a bottle, some of the air inside gets pushed out. But when you're blowing into the bottle, that can't happen. You just blow more air in, and that air pushes the object out.

blowing   piece of paper   air inside

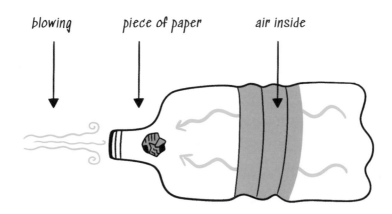

Did you know?

There is actually a way to do it, though. If you blow through a straw, and put it right up against the ball of paper, you may be able to get it in. That's because the air will only blow against the paper, and not around it, into the bottle. This allows some of the air inside the bottle to escape, making space for the ball. Try it!

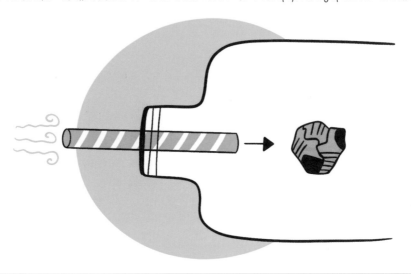

ODD OOBLECK

There's slime ... and then there's super-weird, crazy slime! This bizarrely behaved substance is sometimes called oobleck, and it's quick and easy to make.

The trick

All you need to make oobleck is cornstarch (also called cornflour), and water. Oh, and a splatter-proof space outdoors, or in a kitchen or bathroom, where you can make a mess.

Use a small cup or pot to measure the cornstarch, and place it in a large bowl. Then add 2/3 the amount of water. For example, if you use 6 cups of cornstarch, you'll need 4 cups of water.

cornstarch + 2/3 water = mix!

Slowly stir the oobleck, and mix it with your hand, until you have a thick gloop. Then try these amazing tricks:

- Hit the surface of the oobleck—it's hard! But press it gently, and it's runny!

- Grab a handful and quickly squeeze it—it will form a solid ball. Let go, and it runs away!

- Stand a small plastic figure on the slime and let it sink in. Then try to pull it out quickly. It's stuck fast, as though in quicksand!

Just what exactly is this strange stuff?

solid or liquid?

What's going on?

This mindboggling material has a fancy scientific name—it's a "non-Newtonian fluid." This means that when it's under pressure, its viscosity (or thickness) changes. Squeeze or squash it, and the particles lock together, and act like a solid. Move it slowly and gently, and it's a liquid.

Slurp

Did you know?

People have filled whole paddling pools, or even swimming pools, with oobleck, and tried running across the surface. If they run fast, they stay on top. The second they stop, they sink!

POP ROCKET

It's the one you've been waiting for ... a science trick that goes BANG! With an exciting explosion, your rocket will head for the skies. (Or the ceiling.)

the trick

To make this work, find a small, tube-shaped plastic container with a tight-fitting pop-off top (NOT a screw cap). An old-fashioned camera film canister is perfect, but snacks, vitamins, glitter, and beads often come in this kind of container, too.

You also need some bicarbonate of soda or baking soda, and some vinegar. It's best to do the trick outdoors, as it can get messy.

Pop-off lid

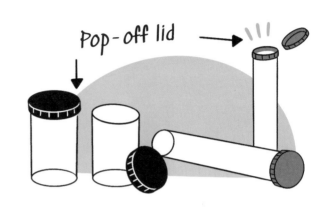

Pour some vinegar into the container until it's about 1/3 full.

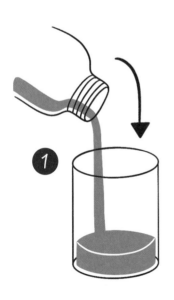

Turn over the lid, and spoon on a little pile of baking soda, in the middle.

Now, as quickly as you can, flip the lid over onto the container, press it on, turn the container upside down, put it on the ground ... and STAND BACK!

WHOOOOSH!

POP!

ZOOOOOM!

What's going on?

This is an example of a chemical reaction. When these two materials mix together, they react, and change, making new substances. One of the new substances is a gas—carbon dioxide. The gas fills the container, increasing the pressure inside of it, and presses against the lid, making the lid pop off. This pushes the container upward, and it shoots off like a rocket.

Did you know?

To make a more realistic rocket, you can roll paper or card around the tube first, and add a pointed nose cone and fins.

INVISIBLE INK

Invisible ink is perfect for sending secret spy messages—such as
"Meet me by the statue at midnight!" or "Don't forget to buy chocolate!"
Luckily, you can do this with everyday household ingredients.

the trick

First, you'll need some lemon juice. You can use lemon juice that comes in a bottle, or use a lemon squeezer
to collect some from a fresh lemon. Just use a thin paintbrush, write your message with the juice on a piece
of white paper, and let it dry completely.

To read the invisible ink message, all your fellow spies have to do is to heat up the paper using a hairdryer. (Ask
an adult's permission before you borrow it!) The ink will gradually turn brown, and the message will be revealed!

What's going on?

Lemon juice, like most foods, contains the element carbon, which is a dark shade.
When it's heated, it reacts with the air, and some of the carbon is released, turning the lemon juice brown.

Why not try?

Several other substances also work as invisible ink. Some spies swear by white vinegar, apple juice, milk, or even onion juice! You could try some of these out, as well as other types of juice, and drinks, and see how well they work.

INVISIBLE WATER

Imagine pouring water onto a lit candle flame. It would go out, right?
This trick does the same thing, but the "water" is invisible!
(And, in case you hadn't guessed, it's not really water!)

The trick

For this trick, you'll need some bicarbonate of soda (baking soda), and vinegar—
every science trickster's best ingredients.

Now, put a few spoonfuls of the baking soda into a jug, and add a similar amount of vinegar. They will react together—fizzing, and bubbling up.

With adult help, place a small candle, such as a tea light, on a heatproof plate or tray, and light it.

With your hand over the top, carefully lift up the jug. Take your hand away, and tilt it a little over the candle flame, as though you were slowly pouring a jug full of water. (Don't tilt it so much that the mixture pours out.) Although you can't see anything, the candle should go out!

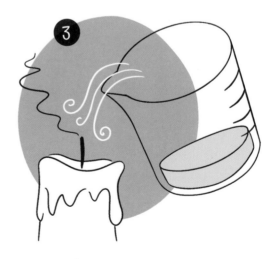

What's going on?

When you combine baking soda and vinegar, they react together, and make carbon dioxide gas.
This invisible gas is heavier than air, so instead of floating away, it collects in the jug. When you pour it, it flows out of the jug, and down onto the candle. Fire needs oxygen from the air to burn. The carbon dioxide pushes the air out of the way, so the candle has no oxygen, and goes out!

Safe and sound!

SHRINKING SNACK BAG

All it takes is a quick bake to turn a plastic snack bag into a tiny, cute version of itself!

Safety warning!
You need to use the oven for this, so make sure you have an adult to help you.

The trick

You'll need an empty plastic snack bag—the brighter the better. Wash it out and dry it, then lay it on a large piece of baking paper or parchment. Wrap it up in the paper and turn the parcel over so it stays flat.

Heat the oven to about 200°C (400°F or gas mark 6). Put the parcel on a baking tray, and ask an adult to put it in the oven. Let it bake for about 3 minutes, then ask an adult take it out.

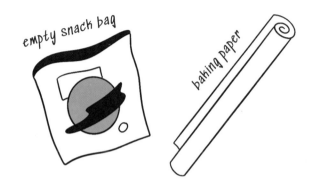

empty snack bag

baking paper

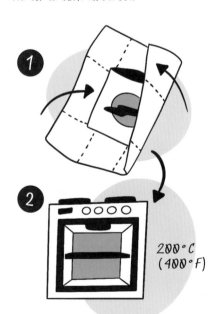

1

2

200°C (400°F)

wait 3 minutes

4

3

flatten

5

It's teeny!

While wearing oven gloves or mitts, press down on top of the parcel to flatten the bag while it's still hot. Then leave it to cool completely, and unwrap it.

What's going on?

This type of plastic bag is made from a substance called a polymer. Polymers are made of molecules joined together in stretchy chains. To make the flat bag material, the polymer is heated and the molecule chains stretch out. Then, as they cool down, they take on that shape.

However, when you heat the plastic again, they pull back into shorter chains again, making the whole bag shrink.

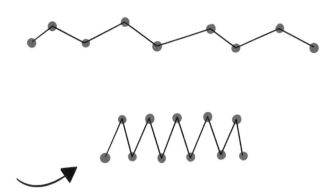

Did you know?

You can make a hole in the shrunken bag with a hole punch, and turn it into a keychain or necklace, or tape a safety pin to the back to make a button.

FROSTY WINDOWS

This sparkly science trick makes icy-looking crystals appear on a window or mirror—even if it's not cold at all!

the trick

The trick works using Epsom salt. Besides the table salt we put on our food, there are many other types of salt, and Epsom salt is one of them. People often put it in their bath to relax their muscles, and you can usually find it in a supermarket or pharmacy.

Find these items to get started:

water

salt

soap

paper towel

1 boil

Ask an adult to boil a teakettle, then half-fill a cup with hot water.

2

Add several tablespoons of Epsom salt, and stir until it dissolves. Squirt in 2 drops of liquid soap, and stir again.

3 dip

Let the mixture cool down a bit. Then dip a cloth or paper towel into the liquid, and spread some across a window or mirror ...

4 window

... as the mixture dries, amazing crystal patterns will appear.

What's going on?

Epsom salt, like table salt, forms in crystal shapes. This happens because of the shapes of its molecules, and the way they fit together. When you dissolve the salt in water, the molecules get separated. Then, as the water dries out and evaporates, the molecules stick back together to form new crystals.

What about the soap? That makes the crystals easier to wipe off afterward!

Did you know?

If you make the same mixture without the soap, and hang a shape made from a pipe cleaner in the liquid, crystals will grow all over it, giving it an icy effect!

Or you can use the liquid to paint a picture on black craft paper. When it dries, it will look like sparkly frost.

HOMEMADE LAVA LAMP

A lava lamp has a light at the bottom, and a container of liquid on top with wax in it.
When you switch it on, the light heats the wax, and it starts moving up and down in the liquid.

the trick

To make your own version, you'll need a clear jar or bottle. Fill it about 1/5 full with water,
and add a few drops of food dye. Then carefully pour oil on top, until the jar is almost full.
You can use any kind of basic cooking oil, such as sunflower or vegetable oil.

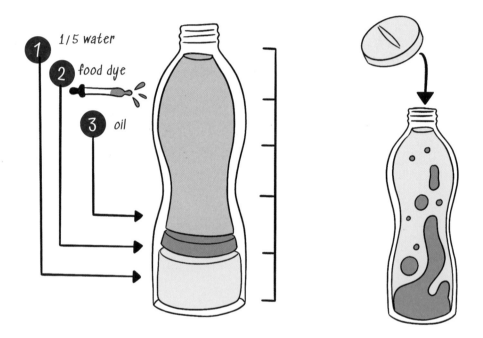

Now you need a fizzy tablet, like a fizzing vitamin tablet. If you don't have one, a chunk of bath bomb
also works. Drop it into the jar, and let it sink to the bottom. When it touches the water, it will start
to fizz and make bubbles, and bright blobs will begin floating up and down.

What's going on?

Oil and water are very different types of liquid, and they don't mix well.
The oil is lighter, and floats on the water. When the tablet makes bubbles in the water, they
rise up through the oil because air is lighter, taking some of the food dye with them.
At the top of the oil, the bubbles pop, and the food dye falls back down.

Did you know?

In a factory-made lava lamp, the light at the bottom makes it glow.
You can add this effect to your lamp by shining a flashlight or torch up through the base.

Did you know?

If you put oil and water in a jar, screw the lid on tightly, and shake it up, they will mix together for a while. But leave them to settle, and they'll separate into two layers again!

Ooohh!

ICE CREAM IN A BAG

Your friends won't believe it when you tell them that you can make instant ice cream in a bag! Here's the recipe ...

The trick

First, you'll need a big bag of ice cubes, and a packet of salt. You can buy bags of ice cubes, or, if you have enough ice-cube trays, make some in the freezer. You also need a small, sealable plastic food bag, milk (or milk substitute, such as soya or oat milk), and sugar.

ice

salt

sugar

bag

milk (or milk substitutes)

1

Pour some milk into the small bag, along with a bit of sugar, and if you like, a drop of vanilla extract.

2

Carefully, seal the bag shut. Then pour the salt into the large bag of ice cubes and stir it in.

3

Quickly place the smaller bag in the bag of ice cubes, close the larger bag, and seal shut.

4

Shake it for a few minutes, then check what's in the small bag. It should be ice cream ... try it!

yum!

Did you know?

**This is also why we put
salt on icy roads.**
It lowers the freezing point, so the ice
melts, and the road is less slippery.

INK FLOWERS

There's more to a marker or pen than meets the eye! This trick reveals what's hiding in the ink—and turns it into a flower pattern!

The trick

You'll need some coffee filter papers, or paper towels, and washable markers or pens.
(Don't use permanent markers—they won't work.)

Cut out circles of filter paper, about 10 cm (4 inches) across. Using one or two markers, draw a ring of dots around the middle of a paper circle, like this:

Now you need a small glass or plastic cup, filled almost to the top with water.

Put your paper circle over it, and press it down in the middle so that it touches the water.

Leave it for a few minutes, and watch the flower appear!

What's going on?

Most pen ink is made of a mixture of different ingredients. When the water soaks into the paper, it spreads out, taking the ink with it. Some of the ink ingredients are less dense, and so travel farther through the paper than others, creating a flower-like pattern.

Did you know?

Scientists call this trick "chromatography," and they actually use it in experiments.
Not to make flowers, but to split substances into separate ingredients, to see what they're made of.

When they're dry, you can cut the circles
into flower shapes, and use them to make
a picture, wall decorations, or a mobile.

MONSTER MARSHMALLOW

How can you make a marshmallow grow to monster size?
Just put it in the microwave. (You'll need an adult to help.)

the trick

Place a plain marshmallow in the middle of a microwaveable plate. Put the plate in the microwave, and cook it on high power for about 30–40 seconds. Look through the window of the microwave to see what happens. It should grow into a monster-sized marshmallow!

1

2 30-60 seconds

3

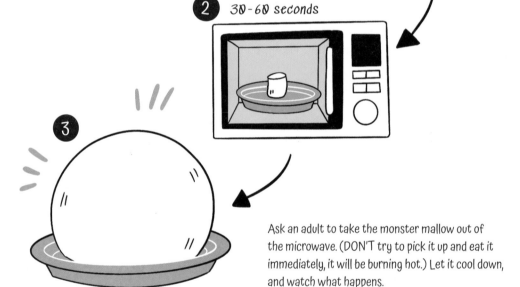

Ask an adult to take the monster mallow out of the microwave. (DON'T try to pick it up and eat it immediately, it will be burning hot.) Let it cool down, and watch what happens.

What's going on?

A marshmallow is made of foam—a solid with lots of air bubbles trapped inside.
When air gets hotter, it expands, and gets bigger—a lot bigger! The expanding air grows inside the marshmallow, and turns it into a monster. When it cools down, the air shrinks again.

BALLOON KEBAB

Challenge your friends to stick a wooden skewer into a balloon
without it popping. (Have a few balloons handy!)

the trick

It may sound impossible, but this trick is easy! You need a blown-up balloon, but make sure it's not TOO full of air. Take a wooden skewer (the type used for kebabs) and gently push it into the balloon, next to the neck, where it's tied. Keep pushing, and guide the point of the skewer to the top of the balloon, where there's a darker spot of thicker rubber. Push it through this point, and there it is—a balloon kebab!

not working:

better:

What's going on?

Balloons pop easily because when the tightly stretched rubber gets pierced, it pulls away quickly, making the balloon collapse and the air rush out. But if you pierce the balloon where the rubber is thick and less stretched out, this doesn't happen. (The air will gradually escape, though.)

HOT AND COLD HANDS

Your body knows when it feels hot or cold, right? Or does it?
Try this amazing trick to find out, then test it on your friends!

The trick

You'll need three large bowls, such as mixing bowls. Fill one with cold water, and one with water from the tap (not too hot to touch). Fill the third with a mixture of hot and cold to make lukewarm water.

Put the three bowls on a table, with the lukewarm one in the middle. Now put one hand in the hot water, and one hand in the cold water. Leave them there for 60 seconds. Then take out both hands and quickly put them both in the bowl of lukewarm water. How does it feel?

hot

cold

lukewarm

What's going on?

If you've followed the steps, you should have a weird sensation that one of your hands is in cold water, and the other is in hot water—even though they're both in the same water!

This is because our bodies aren't actually very good at sensing temperature. We sense temperature differences and contrasts, not exact temperatures. The hand that was in hot water feels cold because it's become used to the hot water, and vice versa.

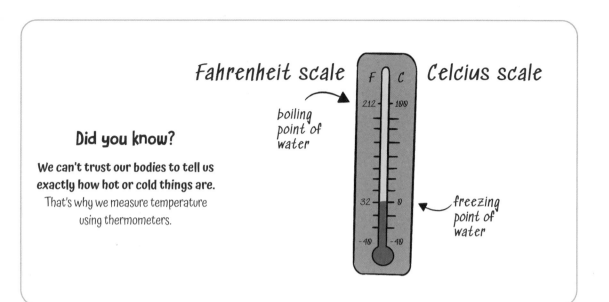

Fahrenheit scale

boiling
point of
water

Celcius scale

freezing
point of
water

Did you know?

**We can't trust our bodies to tell us
exactly how hot or cold things are.**
That's why we measure temperature
using thermometers.

In the snowy mountains in Japan,
these macaques enjoy a nice hot
bath to warm up, just like humans!

ICE FISHING

This trick makes a fun challenge to set your family around the dinner table.
Can they pick up a floating ice cube with a piece of string?

The trick

You'll need a glass or bowl of water with an ice cube floating in it, and a piece of string about 30 cm (12 inches) long. Any kind of thin string or thread will do. The challenge is to use the string to lift the ice cube out of the water, WITHOUT touching the ice cube with your hands.

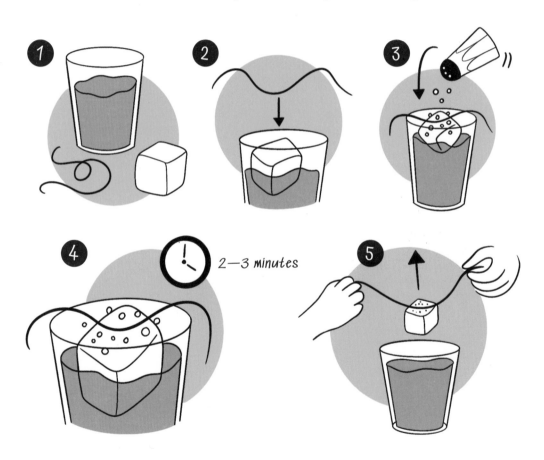

2—3 minutes

However much they try to hook or tie the string around the ice cube, it will slide off. But here's the secret. Place the string across the top of the ice cube, then sprinkle a layer of salt on top. Wait a couple of minutes, then carefully lift up the string—the ice cube should come with it!

What's going on?

Salt reduces the freezing point of water. So when you add salt, the ice at the top of the ice cube starts to melt. The string sinks down into the melted water. But before long, the melting water washes away the salt, and the melted water starts to freeze solid again—this time, with the string stuck into it!

Did you know?

If you're feeling arty, you can watch how salt melts ice with the help of some food dye. Freeze water in a plastic container to make a block of ice, and put it in a tray. Drip some food dye onto the ice, then sprinkle salt on top. The ice will start to melt, forming deep channels, while the dye will sink and spread through them.

THE EGGCELLENT EGG TRICK

Place a hard-boiled egg on top of a glass bottle. Tell everyone you can get the egg to go INSIDE the bottle, without cutting it up. They won't believe you!

BLOOP BLOOP! Safety warning

Ask an adult to help you cook the egg, and when using matches.

The trick

First, prepare your trick.

A glass bottle with a wide opening (slightly narrower than your egg) works best. Sauce bottles are often the right size—just make sure that your bottle is clean and dry inside.

10 minutes!

Ask an adult to help you cook an egg in boiling water for 10 minutes, so that it's hard all the way through.

Let the egg cool, then carefully peel off the shell.

Dip the egg in water to make it damp, then place it on top of the bottle.

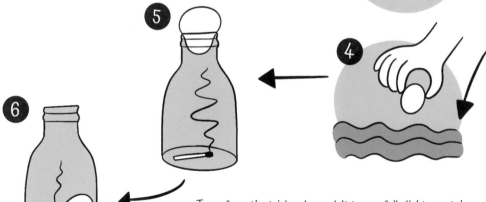

To perform the trick, ask an adult to carefully light a match.

Lift up the egg, then drop the lit match inside the bottle, and quickly put the egg back on top. In it goes!

What's going on?

The trick works because air, like other materials, expands or gets bigger when it heats up, and shrinks when it cools down. The lit match heats the air in the bottle, making it expand. When the match goes out, the air cools down.

And now, for my next trick ...

But now the egg is blocking the opening, so the shrinking air reduces the pressure inside the bottle. The air pressure outside the bottle is stronger, and so the egg is pushed inside the bottle.

BOTTLE FOUNTAIN

Here's another cool trick that uses hot and cold to expand and shrink air.
Create a mini fountain inside a bottle!

the trick

First, fill a large jug 3/4 full with cold water. Add some ice cubes, and a few drops of food dye.
Find a plastic bottle, a straw, and some play dough, or clay. Take a lump of the dough, and form a ball around
one end of the straw. The ball should be big enough to make a tight seal over the opening of the bottle.
Push the straw through the dough, until reaches 3/4 of the way down the bottle, and seal it in place.
Trim off the top end of the straw.

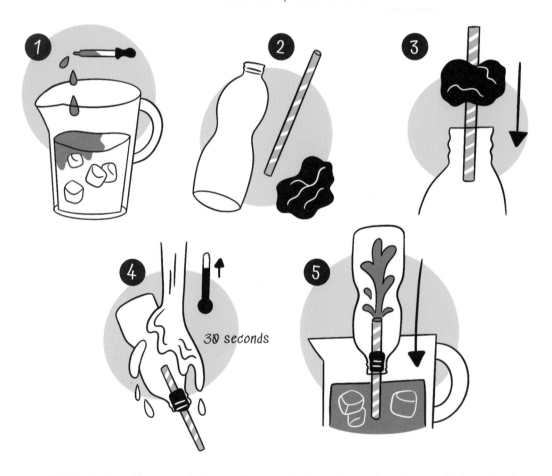

Hold the bottle upside down under hot running water for about 30 seconds, making sure it's heated up all over.
Then quickly plunge the bottle, spout end down, into the iced water mixture—and there's your fountain!

What's going on?

When you heat the bottle, the air inside warms up, too. The air expands, and some of it gets pushed out of the straw. Then, when the bottle hits the cold water, the air inside shrinks suddenly. As it shrinks, the pressure drops. The air pressure outside the bottle is greater than the air pressure inside the bottle, so it pushes the dyed water up the straw, and out of the end!

MARSHMALLOW MELTER

If it's a hot, sunny day, all you need to cook up a treat is a pizza box!
This awesome oven doesn't need any electricity, just the heat of the sun.

the trick

Take a pizza box, or a similar large, flat box with a flap lid. First, cut around the front and sides of the lid, about 2 cm (1 inch) in from the edge, to make a smaller flap, as shown below:

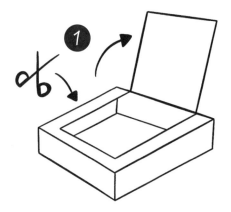

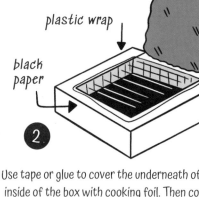

foil

plastic wrap

black paper

Use tape or glue to cover the underneath of the flap and the inside of the box with cooking foil. Then cover the inside of the bottom of the box with black paper, on top of the foil. Lift up the extra flap and cover the hole in the box lid with clear plastic food wrap, stretched out so it's smooth.

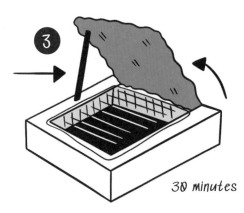

30 minutes

Close the lid, and tape a straw or pencil to prop open the flap, like this.

Place the oven in bright sunshine with the flap facing the sun. Leave it to heat up for about half an hour, then you're ready to cook!

Place a cracker, or sliced lengths of banana on a small piece of foil, and top with a marshmallow, or square of chocolate. Put it inside the oven, under the clear window, and watch what happens!

What's going on?

The silver foil reflects heat from the sun, and directs it inside the box.
The black paper absorbs sunlight and heats up, adding extra heat, while the clear wrap window traps the heat inside. So the inside of the box gets hotter and hotter, like a greenhouse.

Did you know?

You can cook all sorts of tasty treats in your pizza box oven—
try bread with cheese on top, nachos, or slices of apple sprinkled with sugar and cinnamon.

SPINNING SPIRAL

If you have a heater or radiator in your house or classroom,
you can use it to make a spiral spin around on its own, as if by magic!

The trick

Take a large piece of thick or heavy paper, and draw a spiral on it, like the one below. Make the spiral the same thickness all the way from the middle to the edge.

Cut out the spiral, then cut along the line from the edge to the middle. Carefully make a small hole through the middle, using scissors or a sharp pencil.

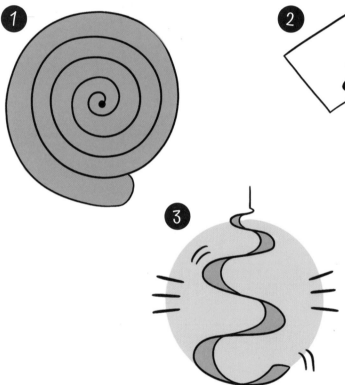

Cut a long piece of string, tie a knot in one end, and thread the other end through the hole, ready to hang.

Then ask an adult to help you hang your spiral above a warm radiator or heater—and watch it go!

What's going on?

When air is heated, it expands and rises, as its molecules spread out away from each other.
Cool air is more dense and sinks. Above a radiator, warm air is rising, and moving upward.
As the warm air hits the bottom of the spiral, it pushes the spiral, making it spin.

Did you know?

Hot and cold air rising and falling, on a much bigger scale, is a big part of how weather works. As hot air rises, cooler air gets sucked in along the ground. And as cold air sinks, it spreads out and flows sideways, making wind!

FLAMEPROOF BALLOON

No one will believe you when you say you can hold a balloon over a candle flame, without making it pop. Challenge them to try it first, and see what happens!

BLOOP BLOOP! Safety warning!

Always ask an adult to help when you're doing tricks that involve candles, matches, or flames.

The trick

You'll need a few medium-sized balloons for this trick, along with a candle.
Place your candle on a flat surface, on a heatproof plate or tray. Then blow up a balloon, and tie the end.

Ask an adult to light the candle, and a friend to see if they can hold it over the flame without it popping. What are the chances? Not good! A bang will follow, as the balloon bursts.

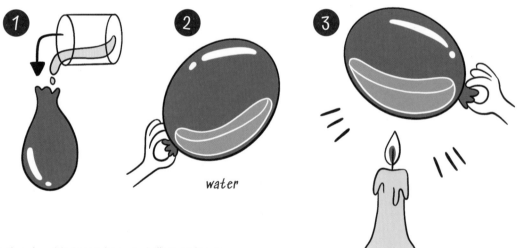

water

To show how it's done, take a new balloon and pour about a cupful of water into it, by holding the opening of the balloon over a tap, or by using a small funnel. Now carefully blow up the balloon, without spilling the water, and tie the end tightly.

Hold the balloon over the candle flame, making sure the water inside the balloon is right over the flame. Does the balloon pop? IT DOES NOT!

What's going on?

The reason this works is that water is very good at absorbing (soaking up) heat.
It takes a lot of heat energy to make water warm up. That's why it takes a long time to boil a big pan of water, and why cold water cools you down when you're hot.

Usually, when a hot candle flame touches a balloon, the intense heat melts a hole in the rubber instantly, making the balloon pop. But, if there's water inside, the water absorbs the heat before the rubber can get hot enough to melt.

THE MAGIC FLAME

Tell your friends that you can light a candle with a match, without the flame touching the wick. It sounds impossible—but with this "magic" trick (actually science!), you can.

BLOOP BLOOP! Safety warning!
It's another candle trick—so always have an adult around to supervise.

The trick

For this trick to work, you'll need to be indoors with still, calm air.
If there's a draft from an open window, or a fan blowing, it will fail!

First, challenge your friends or family to try it. They have to strike a match and use it to light a candle, but the match flame must not touch any part of the candle. It's impossible—to get a candle wick to set alight, you have to touch it with the match's flame for a few seconds.

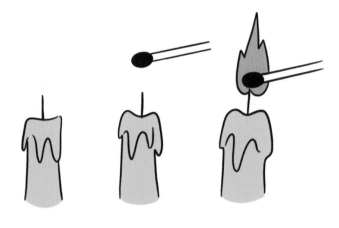

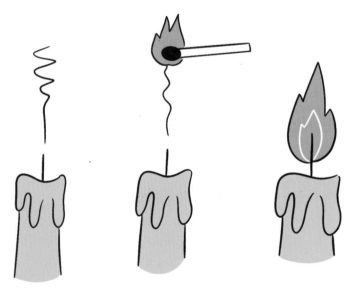

Now it's your turn. Ask an adult to light the candle, and let it burn for a while. Have a match ready, then gently blow the candle out. After it goes out, a thin trail of smoke will rise up from the wick. Carefully strike your match and hold the flame in the smoke trail, above the candle. Ta-da! The candle lights itself again!

What's going on?

When a candle burns, the wax melts, and turns into a hot vapor, or gas. It's this gas that is burning when you see a candle flame. When you blow out the candle, the smoke that rises up from the wick contains some of the leftover hot wax vapor, which burns very easily. If you touch a flame to the smoke, the vapor catches fire ... the fire spreads back down to the wick and lights it again!

CAN CRUSHER

This trick makes a metal drink can IMPLODE in an instant—with the help of heat and cold.

BLOOP BLOOP! Safety warning!

Ask an adult to do the hot parts of this trick, including holding and plunging the hot can!

the trick

First, fill a large bowl with cold water, and stir in some ice cubes. Then you need a clean, empty drink can, an oven, and some long metal tongs.

Ask an adult to heat the oven to its hottest setting. While you are waiting, pour a few teaspoons of the iced water into the can.

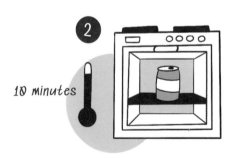

10 minutes

When the oven is hot, ask an adult to put the can inside. After about 10 minutes, the can will be really hot, and the water inside it will begin to boil.

Scrunch!

Ask an adult to remove the hot can from the oven, using the tongs. They should quickly turn the can upside down, and plunge it into the iced water. Watch it go SCRUNCH!

What's going on?

When you heat the can with the water inside, the water boils, and turns from a liquid into a gas—water vapor. Now the can is full of water vapor instead of air.

When the can is plunged upside down into the iced water, the water vapor inside the can instantly cools down and turns back into liquid water. But this takes up much, much less space than the vapor. The pressure inside the can drops, and its entrance is blocked with water so it can't suck in air. In a split second, the greater air pressure outside the can crushes it like a grape!

Did you know?

Heat and cold make water, and many other materials change state, between solid, liquid, and gas. For example, water freezes when it's below 0°C (32°F), and boils and turns into gas at 100°C (212°F).

ICE BALLOONS

This is a great trick to try when the weather outside is freezing!

The trick

Fill a balloon with water, tie the end, and put it outside to freeze. (If it's not cold enough, you could freeze your balloon in a freezer, as long as there's enough space. Ask first!)

When it's frozen solid, cut off the neck of the balloon. You're left with a perfect ice dome. For a winter decoration, put outdoor lights in the snow, and place the ice balloon over the top. The light will shine through it, making an ice-balloon lamp.

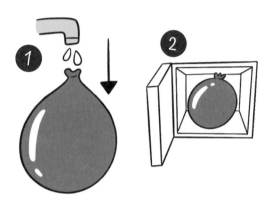

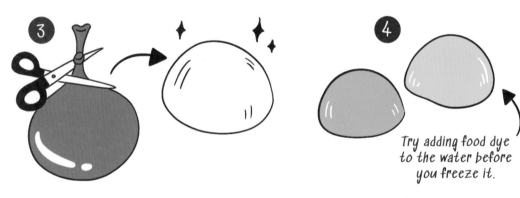

Try adding food dye to the water before you freeze it.

What's going on?

When you fill a balloon with air or water, it pushes out in all directions. The balloon is stretched equally all around, and takes the roundest shape it can.

ICE BUBBLES

Why do bubbles pop so soon? Well, they don't if you freeze them!

The trick

When it's below freezing outdoors, here's how to make a bubble last.

Take some bubble mixture outside and blow a large bubble. Catch it on your bubble wand and hold it still. If you're lucky, you'll see crystal patterns forming across the bubble, as it freezes solid.

If it's not that cold, pour some bubble mixture onto a small ceramic plate and blow into it using a straw to make a half-bubble. Carefully put the plate and bubble in the freezer, and leave it to freeze.

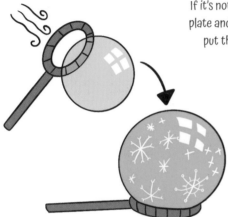

What's going on?

A bubble is made of a thin film of soap.
As the air inside pushes out in all directions, it forms a sphere. But as gravity pulls the liquid soap down to the bottom of the bubble, the top becomes too thin, and it bursts. If you freeze a bubble, this can't happen, and the bubble lasts longer.

Tip: Try breaking a frozen bubble, and see how thin the soap layer is.

MAKE A GLASS DISAPPEAR!

Simply show your friends a small glass, and tell them you're going to make it vanish before their very eyes! (You might want to check you can definitely make it work beforehand, though!)

the trick

As well as a small glass, you'll need a larger glass jug or bowl that the glass can fit inside, and a bottle of cooking oil, such as sunflower oil (ask an adult first before using). Put the glass inside the jug or bowl, and check that everyone can see it.

Then slowly pour oil into the bowl until it fills up and covers the glass. Abracadabra—the glass is gone!

What's going on?

This trick works because of the way light bends, or refracts, as it shines through transparent objects. When you look at a glass, you're seeing beams of light that have shone through it. As light passes in and out of different clear materials, such as glass or water, it bends and changes direction.

That's why things look bent and distorted when you look at them through a glass bowl, for example. The light that reaches your eyes has been bent on its way through.

Some clear materials refract light more than others. But glass and oil are very similar in this way. When the glass is in the oil, light hardly bends at all as it passes from the oil into the glass and out again. So you can't see where the glass is hiding!

Did you know?

Why doesn't this happen when you look through a window?
It does! Because the glass is flat, most objects don't look
very different, but they are slightly distorted.

YOUR ROOM IS A CAMERA!

Have you ever wondered how a camera works? It captures an image by letting in light rays through a small hole. You can do the same in your own room!

The trick

It works best with a room that has pale walls, and a small window that's easy to cover up.
The window should also have a view of something—not just the sky, for example.

With an adult to help, cover the window with old cardboard boxes, black trash bags, or thick black fabric.
Stick it down around the edges with removable tape to stop any light escaping.
Then make a small hole in the cardboard, plastic, or fabric, using scissors or a sharp pencil.

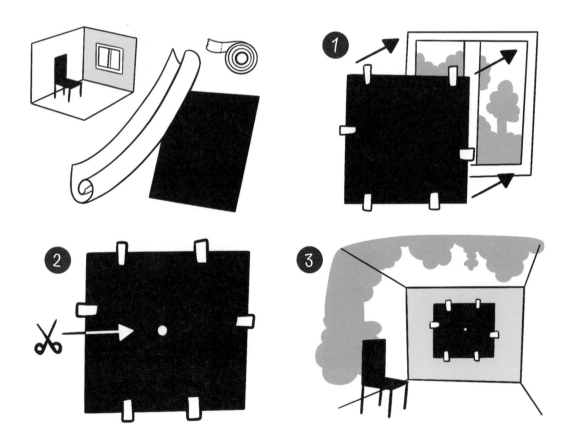

In bright daylight, with all the lights in the room switched off, and the door closed, the camera should work. Look at the wall opposite the window, and see if you can see an image of the outside world. It will be upside down!

What's going on?

Everything outside the room is reflecting light in all directions. But only narrow beams of light can shine through the small hole. Light beams travel in straight lines. So as each beam of light enters the hole, it keeps going and hits the wall on the opposite side of the hole from where it started. This makes a picture of the outside world on the opposite wall, but the wrong way up and back to front!

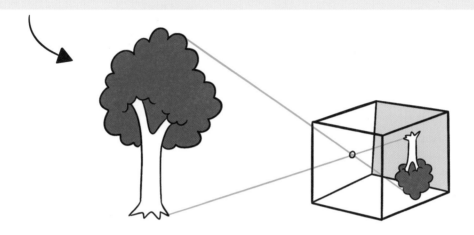

Did you know?

This ancient trick is called a camera obscura, which is Latin for "dark room"!

PAINTING WITH LIGHT

Have you ever waved a sparkler or a glow stick around in the dark so fast, it seems to leave a trail of light? It's like painting with light! Here's how to make your paintings permanent with a phone camera.

the trick

You'll need a glow stick or other small light, phone camera, a dark night or a dark room, and an adult to help. Ask the adult to help set the camera to a long shutter speed. This makes the camera take a single picture over a longer time, such as 10 seconds. (If the camera doesn't have this function, look for an app that does.)

glow sticks

camera or app

In the dark, ask the adult to take the photo, while you wave the light around to make patterns and shapes. When you look at the photo, you'll see all the lines you "painted" as you moved!

What's going on?

A light source, such as a glow stick, gives out a constant stream of light energy.
In your eyes, the light energy gets turned into signals that are sent to your brain. You only sense each bit of light for a short time. If a light source is moving fast, you may see a short trail of light.

However, a camera captures and stores light as a fixed image. Wherever the light is, the camera records it, and adds it to the picture. As the rest of the image is dark, all you see is a "light painting."

Did you know?

You can create loads of arty effects using different lights—try fairy lights, flashing bicycle lights, or a glowing bedside light, or even another phone with a glowing screen.

GLOW IN THE DARK

These days you can buy sugar in all shapes and sizes, but in the olden days, sweetening your coffee was more complicated. People had to buy a big, hard lump of sugar called a "sugar loaf" and chip bits off. If they did this in the dark, they sometimes saw a flash of light!

The trick

You can recreate this amazing effect with some sugar cubes or sugary mints. You'll need a very dark room, a clear food bag, a large pair of pliers, and an adult to help.

First, place a few sweets inside the bag and seal it up. Take everything into the dark room, and ask the adult to use the pliers to CRUSH the mints or sugar cubes through the bag. (The bag catches the bits, so you don't make a mess.)

Watch carefully as each mint or sugar cube is crushed. Can you see flashes of glowing greenish-blue light?

What's going on?

Light comes from sources such as the sun, a bedside lamp, a candle flame, or even a glowing firefly.
Light is a type of energy, and it can only be made from another type of energy. For example, in a candle, the wax is a fuel because it contains chemical energy. It makes light as it burns. A bedside lamp turns electrical energy into light.

As the sugar cubes are crushed, the energy from this movement becomes light. This type of light has its own name—"triboluminescence." But how does it work? Err—we'll get back to you on that! (Scientists aren't really sure!)

Did you know?

There are some other ways of creating triboluminescence, too. Try quickly pulling tape off a roll, pulling the backing off a sticking plaster or bandage, or ripping open a sticky envelope seal. You can also make a mint or sugar cube glow in your mouth by crunching it!

BEND A LASER BEAM

When you point at the floor or wall with a laser pointer, a dot appears exactly where you're pointing, as light travels in straight lines. So how you can make a laser beam curve around a corner?

BLOOP BLOOP! Safety warning!

Laser pointers can cause permanent damage to your eyesight when not used safely.
Read and follow these safety tips when using laser pointers, and ask an adult to supervise at all times.

- Before turning on the laser pointer, make sure that it is pointed away from yourself and others.
- Never aim or shine a laser directly at any person, or animal, or at any shiny or reflective surface.

The trick

You'll need a laser pointer or laser cat toy, along with a large clear plastic bottle, a bowl or bucket, a chair, tape, and sharp scissors.

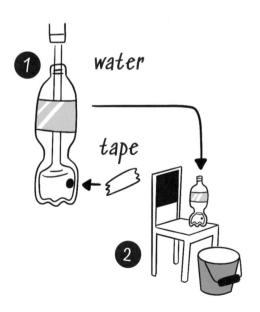

First, ask an adult to make a small hole in the bottle, about 8 cm (3 inches) from the bottom, using scissors. Cover the hole with tape, then fill the bottle with water, and screw on the lid.

Stand the bottle on the chair, with the bowl or bucket positioned on the floor to catch the water.

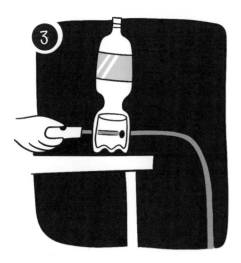

Turn off the lights, and shine the laser pointer through the side of the bottle opposite the hole, pointing it at the hole. Now remove the bottle lid, and the tape.

The water should flow out of the bottle in a long, curved stream. If you aim the laser pointer through the hole, the beam of light will follow the flow of water, and curve downward. And if you put your hand under the stream, you'll see the laser light on your hand!

What's going on?

As the laser beam travels through the hole, it is reflected off the inside of the water stream, and changes direction. It bounces to and fro inside the water stream in a zigzag. So it gets carried along with the water, even when it curves.

Did you know?

Fiber-optic cables work like this, too, but instead of water, the light bounces along inside very thin, flexible tubes of glass.

TINY FRIENDS

Imagine how cool it would be to have a friend who could fit on the palm of your hand!
Now, with the help of a camera, you can create the illusion of having a pocket-sized pal.

The trick

**All you need is a camera or smartphone and a large, flat, open space,
like a beach, sports field, or schoolyard—plus a friend and an everyday object,
such as a ball, water bottle, or shoe.**

Ask your friend to stand far away, then put the object on the ground, close to you.

Now get down close to the ground, so that your friend's feet line up with the top of the object.
Your friend is much farther away and will look tiny, but if you get the angle exactly right,
you can take a photo that makes it look like a normal object with a tiny person standing on it!

What's going on?

This is all about perspective—how things look when they are nearer or farther away.
When an object is farther away, the beams of light that come from it travel farther to get to your eyes.
This makes a smaller angle as the light beams enter your eyes, and the object or person looks smaller to you.

Of course, you don't think they've suddenly shrunk, because you know they're far away,
but in a photo you can make the tiny person look closer, creating a cool effect.

Did you know?

You can use the same method to create all kinds of funny pictures.
What about a friend being chased by a giant robot or a dragon? (In reality
just a toy!) Or sitting on another friend's head?

WATER FLIP

Tell your friends that you can draw an arrow on a piece of paper,
then make it change direction—WITHOUT touching or moving the paper.

The trick

Find a clear glass or jar with straight, vertical sides. Draw a sideways-pointing arrow on a small piece
of paper, then tape it to the outside of the glass, facing inward. Ask your friends to look through the glass
at the arrow. Then, as they watch, pour water into the glass until it's full. Ta-da!

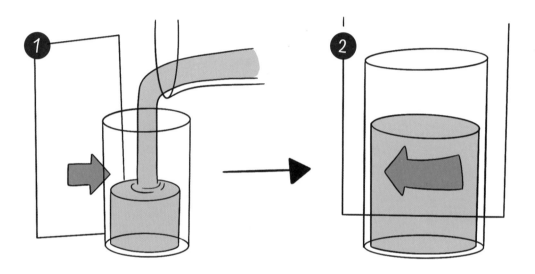

What's going on?

**When you look at the arrow through
the glass, the light coming from it is
refracted a little bit.** But when you add
water, it refracts and bends the light rays
much more—so much that they cross over
each other before they get to your eyes.
This makes the arrow appear to flip,
and point the other way!

SEEING SOUNDS

Do you want to see what it looks like when you sing? Try this!

The trick

First you'll need a round plastic tub, such as an old food tub, and a toilet paper tube. Draw around the end of the tube onto the side of the tub, ask an adult to cut out the hole, and fit the tube through it. Stretch plastic food wrap over the top of the tub and hold it on with an elastic band. Then sprinkle fine powder, such as ground cinnamon or powdered (icing) sugar, onto the plastic wrap.

Now, holding the tub still, sing long notes into the tube. The powder will arrange itself into different patterns for different notes!

What's going on?

Sound happens when things vibrate. To sing, you vibrate the vocal cords in your throat, and this makes the air in the tub and the food wrap vibrate. Different notes make the food wrap vibrate in different places, and the powder collects where it is vibrating the least.

SPRINGY SOUND EFFECTS

Pneeeoouww! Zzwwappp! Have you ever wondered how they make sci-fi sound effects for movies, TV, and videogames? Try this low-tech effect at home!

The trick

For this, you'll need a metal spring toy, and a paper cup. Turn the cup upside down, and ask an adult to help cut a small slot in the base. Thread one end of the metal spring through the slot, so that it lies flat against the base of the cup, and hold it in place with strong tape.

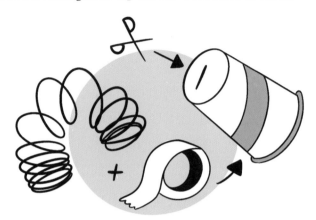

Now simply put the cup to your ear, and shake the spring, bounce it up and down or tap it with a metal spoon. You'll be amazed at the space-age noises it makes!

What's going on?

As the spring moves, it vibrates, making a sound. Usually, you can't hear it very well, but when you attach the cup, it vibrates too, and this makes the air inside vibrate. The cup's cone shape directs the vibrations toward your ear, making them sound much louder.

The reason the sounds are so weird is that the vibrations change, speeding up and slowing down as the spring bounces and stretches.

Did you know?

You can even make a sci-fi voice changer by attaching another paper cup onto the other end of the spring. Hold it to your ear while someone else speaks into it!

STRAW TROMBONE

No trombone of your own? Don't worry—you can make an instrument
in an instant (just slightly smaller than a real trombone!).

The trick

You can make a musical sound with a plastic straw, if you know how. First, flatten the tip of the straw,
then cut it into a point, as shown below. Put the pointed end in your mouth, and bite the straw gently with your
front teeth, about 2 cm (1 inch) from the pointed end. Blow gently, and ...PARP!

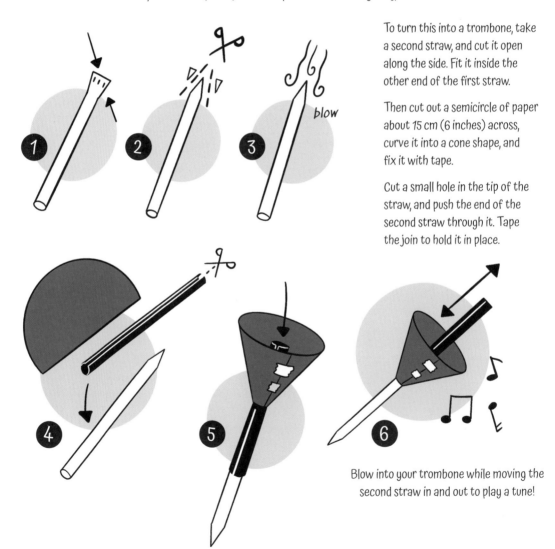

To turn this into a trombone, take
a second straw, and cut it open
along the side. Fit it inside the
other end of the first straw.

Then cut out a semicircle of paper
about 15 cm (6 inches) across,
curve it into a cone shape, and
fix it with tape.

Cut a small hole in the tip of the
straw, and push the end of the
second straw through it. Tape
the join to hold it in place.

Blow into your trombone while moving the
second straw in and out to play a tune!

What's going on?

When you blow into the straw, the two ends of the pointed tip vibrate and buzz against each other. This makes the air in the tube vibrate, too. When the tube is longer, it vibrates more slowly, making a lower note, and vice versa.

Did you know?

Real trombones don't actually work quite like this. With a trombone, it's your lips that vibrate. But woodwind instruments, such as oboes and clarinets, work exactly like this—they have a reed that vibrates in the same way as the end of the straw.

HOMEMADE PHONE SPEAKER

You can plug a phone into an electric speaker to play music—
or make this fabulous homemade version. No batteries required!

The trick

You'll need a long cardboard tube, two paper cups, and a smartphone or tablet.
Hold the end of phone against the middle of the tube and draw around it.

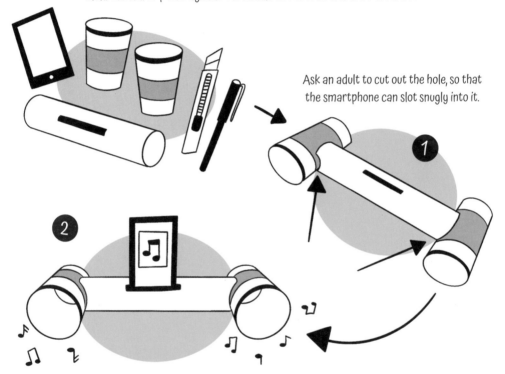

Ask an adult to cut out the hole, so that
the smartphone can slot snugly into it.

Hold one end of the tube against the side of one of the paper
cups. Draw around it, cut out the hole, and fit the tube into it.
Repeat for the second cup, and place on the other end.

Now switch on some music! Make sure the
phone's speaker is on the end of the phone
that's stuck into the tube, and the cups are
pointing toward you. Disco time!

What's going on?

**The vibrations from the phone's small speaker pass into the tube and the cups, and the air
inside them.** The cups make the sound come out in one direction, toward you, so the music sounds louder.

Did you know?

Long before computers and electric speakers, people used to listen to music on records, played on wind-up gramophones. The sound came out of a large horn.

BENDY WATER

What invisible, magical force can pull a stream of water sideways without touching it? The answer is electricity—static electricity!

The trick

You'll need a small plastic object, such as a comb. Rub it up and down on your hair (or on a wool sweater or blanket) for a few seconds.

Then go to the sink and turn on the tap to a straight, narrow stream. Hold your comb to one side of the stream of water, and, without touching it, the water will bend toward it.

What's going on?

Static electricity is an electric charge that builds up in an object. Instead of flowing along a wire like current electricity, it stays still (or "static"). This usually happens in materials that are not good at letting electricity flow through them, like plastic.

When you rub the plastic on your hair, teeny tiny particles called "electrons" get rubbed off your hair and onto the comb. This means the comb has extra electrons. Electrons have a negative, or "-" charge, while water has a positive, or "+" charge. Just like with magnets, opposites attract, so the water pulls toward the comb.

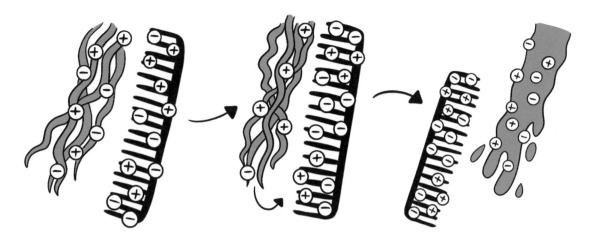

Before the hair is combed there are an equal number of protons and electrons in the hair and on the comb.

While the hair is being combed, electrons move from the hair to the plastic comb.

The comb now has a static charge, and will draw non-charged materials—such as water—toward it.

Did you know?

An ancient Greek scientist named Thales discovered this effect when he rubbed a piece of amber on cat fur. He found that the rubbed amber pulled tiny objects, such as seeds, toward it.

It works with cats' fur, too!

Meow?!

ROLLING-CAN RACE

The power of static can also make an empty can roll along by itself.

The trick

For this, you'll need an inflated balloon, and a clean, empty drink can. Charge the balloon with static electricity by rubbing it on your hair (if you don't mind a bad-hair day!), a wool sweater, or a blanket.

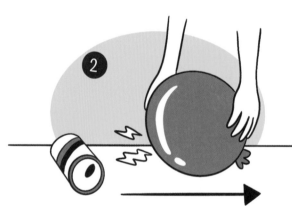

Put the can on its side on a table or on a flat, smooth floor, and hold the balloon near it. It will start to roll toward the balloon. Keep moving the balloon so that the can doesn't touch it, and the can will keep going. How fast can you make it roll?

To have a race, give each person their own balloon and can, and set up a start and finish line. Who can get their can to the finish first? 3, 2, 1, GO!

What's going on?

As in the water-bending trick, the rubbing gives the balloon extra electrons, and a negative static electric charge. This makes it attract (or pull on) the particles in the can that have a positive charge. The can is very light, and it doesn't take much force to make it roll along, so you can make it go quite fast.

Did you know?

When you rub a balloon on your hair, you'll also find it attracts your hair, making it stick up. As the balloon gets extra electrons from your hair, your hair loses electrons. The balloon has a negative charge and your hair has a positive charge, so they attract each other.

LEVITATING CEREAL

Build a levitation chamber, and watch your cereal leave the ground!

the trick

You'll need a shallow metal tray, such as a baking tray, kitchen foil, toilet paper tubes, and a large, clear plastic lid, like the kind that comes with plastic food storage containers. You'll also need some puffed cereal—puffed rice works well.

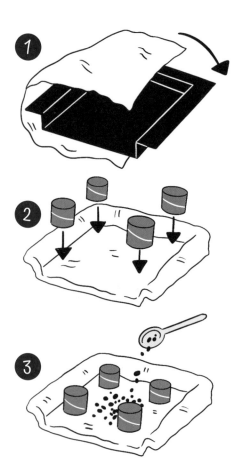

First, use foil to line the tray. Place a layer of foil all over the base, sides, and rim of the tray, and press it down.

Next, cut four pieces of cardboard tube that are tall enough to stick up slightly out of the tray. Stand them in the corners of the tray (or around the edge, if it's round!)

Now sprinkle some cereal into the middle of the tray.

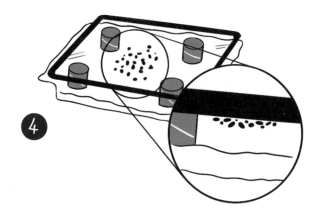

Take the plastic lid, and rub it on your hair or on a wool sweater for 30 seconds to charge it with static. Carefully put it down onto the four cardboard tubes, making sure that it doesn't touch the foil. The cereal will jump up and hang below the lid!

What's going on?

The lid gains electrons, and has a negative charge, which attracts the positive particles in the cereal. The cereal jumps up, and hangs from the lid—but it's also collecting charge from the lid, so some pieces may jump up and down, or even hang in mid-air for a second!

Did you know?

If you touch the top of the lid, your finger will make the cereal dance and scoot around. Why do you think this happens?

LITTLE TINY LIGHTNING

Lightning is a powerful blast of energy from the sky that can destroy
buildings, set fire to forests, and even injure people with an electric shock.
But did you know that it's a kind of static electricity?

The trick

**You can make your own tiny (and
much safer!) lightning spark
with just a balloon, a spoon, and a
dark room.** Blow up the balloon, tie it,
and rub it on a sweater or blanket for
30 seconds to build up static change.

Hold the balloon in one hand and a metal spoon in the other (make sure they don't touch).
Go into a dark room, and slowly move the spoon and the balloon together until they are
almost touching. You should see a spark like a tiny lightning bolt jump across the gap.

What's going on?

When electrons collect in an object that doesn't conduct electricity well, they build up in one place, creating an electric charge. If the object touches a material that does conduct electricity well, the extra electrons can flow into it and spread out.

If there's a strong enough charge, the electrons can actually flow through the air, jumping across the gap. As they flow, they heat up the air and make a spark that you can see.

Did you know?

Lightning happens when the clouds build up electric charge, as they move around in the sky—until a huge spark jumps between the clouds and the ground. If there's an object on the ground, such as a tree, a tower, or a person, the electrons can sometimes flow through that, too, which we call being "struck by lightning." That's why you shouldn't stand on top of a hill during a thunderstorm!

THE FLYING RING

Be warned—this static trick is tricky! So practice it first,
before you use it to amaze your friends.

The trick

First, cut a strip from the middle of a small plastic food bag. Cut across the middle of the bag, so that you end up with a ring of thin plastic. Place it on a flat surface, and rub it with a towel or wool sweater for about 30 seconds to charge it with static.

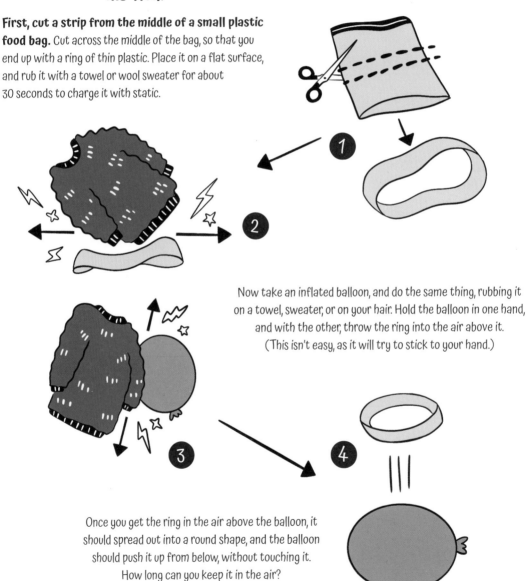

Now take an inflated balloon, and do the same thing, rubbing it on a towel, sweater, or on your hair. Hold the balloon in one hand, and with the other, throw the ring into the air above it. (This isn't easy, as it will try to stick to your hand.)

Once you get the ring in the air above the balloon, it should spread out into a round shape, and the balloon should push it up from below, without touching it. How long can you keep it in the air?

What's going on?

In this trick, you charge both the balloon and the plastic ring with extra electrons, and give them both a negative charge. Matching charges push away from, or "repel" each other, so the balloon pushes the ring away. The plastic in the ring also pushes away from itself, making it spread out into a ring.

UPSIDE-DOWN GRAVITY

Tie a paper clip to a string, hold the string, and the paper clip will dangle down, right?
But you can make it defy gravity, and dangle UP—with the help of a strong magnet.

the trick

First you'll need a medium-sized cardboard box, like a shoebox, without the lid. Make a hole through one side of the box using scissors, or a sharp pencil.

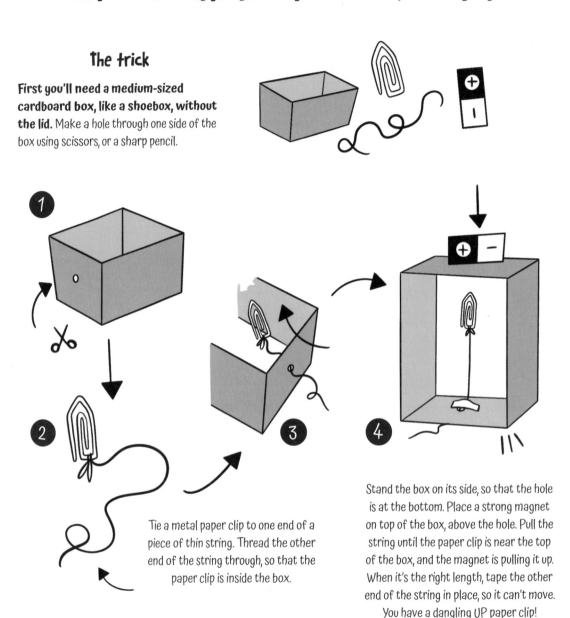

Tie a metal paper clip to one end of a piece of thin string. Thread the other end of the string through, so that the paper clip is inside the box.

Stand the box on its side, so that the hole is at the bottom. Place a strong magnet on top of the box, above the hole. Pull the string until the paper clip is near the top of the box, and the magnet is pulling it up. When it's the right length, tape the other end of the string in place, so it can't move. You have a dangling UP paper clip!

What's going on?

What makes a magnet work? It's all to do with the forces between atoms, the tiny units that make up materials. In most materials, these forces point in all directions. In a magnet, they all pull the same way. This makes a big pulling force that can pull on another object, like the paper clip.

It only works in a few materials though, including the metals iron, steel (which is mostly made of iron), and nickel. So this trick will only work with a metal paper clip.

Did you know?

You can now try doing some tests on your paper clip. How far or hard do you have to push the paper clip, or pull on the string, before the paper clip escapes from the magnet's pull? What happens if you move the magnet? What happens if you use a rubber band instead of a paper clip?

WHICH WAY IS NORTH?

Over 2,000 years ago, people in ancient China discovered something amazing.
If they let a lodestone, a naturally magnetic rock, hang freely, it would
turn itself around so that its two opposite ends pointed north and south.

the trick

First, take a sewing needle and a magnet. Holding the needle still, rub the magnet along it,
in one direction only, about 50 times. This will magnetize the needle, or make it into a magnet.

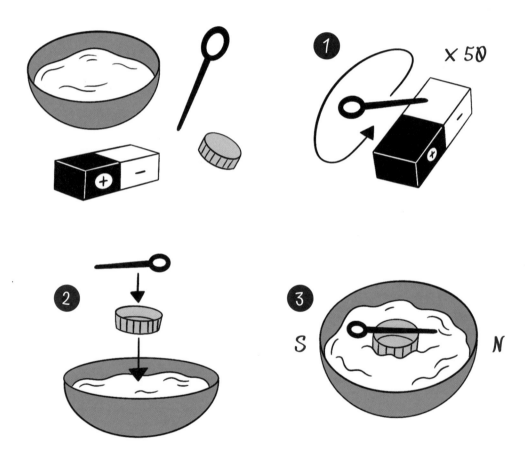

Next, fill a shallow, wide bowl with water and float a small plastic lid or a piece of craft foam in it,
like a little boat. Carefully lay the magnetized needle down across the middle. Wait until the water
is calm, and the two ends of the needle should turn to point north and south.

What's going on?

Magnets, and magnetized objects, will always line themselves up north and south if they can. That's because the Earth is magnetic!

The way melted rocks and metals swirl around inside the Earth makes the planet into a giant magnet. Magnets have two ends, known as the north and south poles. Sound familiar? The Earth's north and south poles attract the opposite ends of a magnet.

A compass has a magnetic needle, and is marked with the compass points. If you line up north with the way the needle is pointing, you can see which way all the directions are.

That way!

Did you know?

At first, the Chinese didn't use their discovery for sailing, but for planning where to build houses. Eventually though, people realized magnets could be used for navigating out at sea and began making portable versions.

MAGNET PAINTING

Want to see a painting paint itself, as if by magic?
This trick uses a magnet to make it happen.

the trick

You'll need a magnet, and a piece of thick or heavy white paper that won't bend easily. Place a metal paper clip on the paper, or use another small metal object, such as a button or safety pin (check to make sure it sticks to a magnet first).

Next, you'll need some thick paint, such as poster paint. Dab several blobs of paint on different parts of the paper, with one blob right on top of your paper clip.

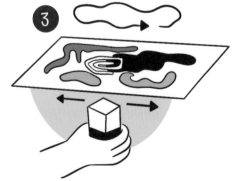

Hold a strong magnet under the paper, where the paper clip is. Now move the magnet around. It will make the paper clip move, dragging paint with it and painting lines. Move the paper clip through the other blobs of paint to mix up the shades, and create magnetic art!

What's going on?

A magnet can pull on a metal object, even if there's another material in the way, like the thick or heavy paper in this experiment.

However, it only works if the material in between is not too thick, and is not a magnet, or a magnetic metal. See what other materials you can get a magnet to work through—fabric, paper, a cracker, or even your hand?

MAGNETIC LEVITATION

If you have two matching magnets, you'll find that depending on which way around you hold them, they either attract each other, and pull together, or repel each other, and push apart. You can use repulsion to make a magnet levitate!

The trick

This trick works best if you can get two ring-shaped magnets. Hold the magnets together and flip them over to discover which sides repel or push away from each other. Place both the magnets onto a pencil, with their repelling sides facing each other.

Hold up the pencil, while holding the lower magnet still. The upper magnet will float or levitate above it. If you try to push it down, it will boing back up!

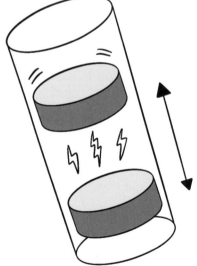

If you don't have ring-shaped magnets, it can also work with disk-shaped magnets— look for a clear tube that they can just fit inside. They need to fit so that they are free to move up and down, without flipping over.

What's going on?

A magnet has two poles, or ends, known as north and south. As with static electricity, opposites attract. So the north end, or side if it's a ring or disc magnet, will attract the north end or side of another magnet. If you put two south poles or two north poles together, they will repel or push apart.

Did you know?

A "maglev" train uses magnetic levitation (the clue's in the name!). Magnetic repulsion makes the train float above the track, so it glides along easily.

MAGNET CHAIN

As you know by now, a metal paper clip will stick to a magnet.
But did you know that it can pass on the magnetism to a whole chain of clips?

The trick

You'll need a magnet and plenty of metal paper clips. Hold up the magnet, then place a paper clip near to it, and it will stick on. Now place another paper clip at the bottom of the first one. It should cling on as well!

Keep adding more and more paper clips. They will hang down in a chain, even though only the first one is touching the magnet.

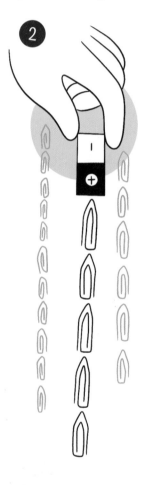

Now pull the top paper clip away from the magnet, and see what happens!

What's going on?

When a magnet attracts a metal object, it pulls on the atoms inside it, so that they all point the same way. This turns the object into a magnet, too. The magnetism is passed on to each paper clip in the chain.

MAGNETIC SHOW

Put on a show for your friends on a magical magnetic stage!

the trick

Glue or tape metal paper clips to the feet or undersides of small toy figures and animals (don't use your best ones!). Place them on a "stage" made of a sheet of stiff, smooth card (cardstock), and move magnets around underneath to bring the characters to life!

You could use cardboard boxes to make a complete model playhouse, with walls around the stage, and a space underneath so you can reach in from behind with the magnets. Try taping your magnets to long sticks.

Can you use magnetic repulsion to make a character jump or fall over?

What's going on?

A magnetic stage like this uses magnets to make things move—magnets are often used this way in toys. They have hundreds of other everyday uses, too. Can you think of some?

GOING DOWN

Trick a friend's brain to make them feel a weird, impossible sensation—
or ask them to do it to you!

The trick

The person you're showing the trick to should lie face down on the floor, with their arms stretched out in front of them. Tell them to relax, and close their eyes. Now take hold of their hands, and gently pull them up, so that their arms, head, and upper body lift off the floor. (It may be easier if you have two people to gently do this, one for each arm.)

Hold the person's arms up for about a minute, then start slowly lowering them back down. As they get lower, the person will feel as though they are falling right through the floor!

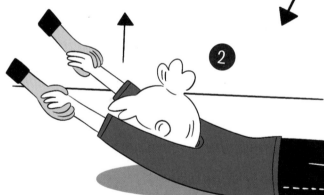

What's going on?

Your brain knows where your body is thanks to a special sense called "proprioception."
Sensors all over your body send signals to your brain telling it what position you're in. When your arms are lifted up, your brain senses that happening. But when they stay there for a minute, it stops noticing the signals. Then, when you move back down, it feels to your brain as though you must be going lower than you actually are. Your brain knows the floor is there, so it decides you must be going through it!

Did you know?

Your brain doesn't get things right every time. There's so much information being sent from all your senses that there's only so much your brain can handle. Instead, it makes guesses, and assumptions based on previous experiences, and sometimes it's mistaken.

SEEING THINGS

Have you ever felt like you were seeing things that aren't really there?
Well, perhaps you did—but it was just your eyes playing tricks on you!

The trick

For this trick, all you have to do is to stare at the picture to the right, without moving your eyes at all, for about one minute. To make sure you keep your eyes in exactly the same position, focus on the little girl's nose.

When 60 seconds are up, quickly look at the empty space at the top of the next page—what do you see?

If you thought that was weird, try this. Copy the spiral pattern below onto a circle of paper, and stick a pencil through the middle.

Stare at the middle of the spiral while turning the pencil around and around, so that the spiral slowly spins. After 60 seconds, look at the back of your hand.

What's going on?

This effect is called an after-image.
When you look at something, light coming from the object enters your eye, and triggers the light-detecting cells at the back of your eyeball. If you keep looking at the same thing for a long time, the cells get used to being triggered by a particular shade or pattern, and become less sensitive.

Then, when you look at blank paper, your eyeball sees the opposite of what it was looking at before—just for a short while. So you see the opposite of the black and white image.

With the spinning spiral, the spiral appears to grow, or shrink, depending on which way you rotate it. Your eyeball gets used to this. Then, when you look at your hand, your brain thinks it can see the opposite thing happening—even though nothing is moving!

TASTE SENSATION!

Think it's easy to tell one food from another? You may be surprised!

The trick

You'll need three foods with a similar texture, like apple, carrot, and cabbage. Keeping them separate, carefully chop the fruit and veg into tiny pieces, then place each food in a bowl.

The person taking the taste test should not see the food being prepared. Sit them at a table and put a blindfold on them, then give them a spoon, and the three bowls. Ask them to hold their nose, then taste the three foods and tell you which is which. Can they do it?

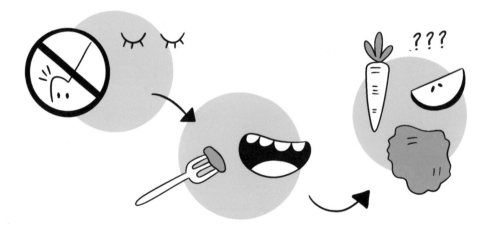

What's going on?

Most people find it really hard to get this right! This is because when you sense things, you don't usually use just one sense. Your other senses back up what you're experiencing, helping you to decide what's happening.

This is especially true with the sense of taste. When you eat, you use your nose to detect the chemicals in the food, as well as your taste buds. Without your nose, many foods just taste the same.

Did you know?

If a familiar food such as bread, or pasta, is dyed blue, most people won't want to eat it—even if it tastes exactly the same. Your brain decides it doesn't look right, and makes you think "Nope!"

MEMORY GENIUS

Challenge your friends or family to this memory test,
but don't tell them your secret!

The trick

First, collect 10 small, everyday household objects, like the ones in this picture. Place them on a tray, and cover them with a cloth.

To test someone, give them a pencil and a piece of paper. They must look at the 10 objects for 30 seconds, then try to remember as many as possible.

When they are ready, reveal the objects, then after 30 seconds, cover them up again. Once they are covered, the person can start writing down the names of the objects they remember.

How did they do? Most people find this game far from easy!

What's going on?

Why is it hard for the brain to remember 10 simple things, when it has thousands and thousands of things in its memory? The reason is that we have two different kinds of memory—short-term and long-term. Short-term memory can't hold very much information at once, and it forgets details quickly unless they are important to you. Important things, and things you experience over and over again, get transferred to your long-term memory.

However, there is a trick to help you do better at this test. When you see the objects, quickly make up a little story that includes them all. It's easier to remember things that are linked together, and have a meaning. When you repeat the story in your head, you'll remember the objects more easily.

For example:

Teddy went out in the sunshine (**sunglasses**), but fell in a lake (**water bottle**), so went home to her **brick** house. She couldn't find her **key**, so she picked the lock with a **twig**. Then she made a **cup of tea**, stirred it with a **spoon**, and sat down to eat an **apple**, and read her **book**.

MISSING VISION

This trick is a bit different—it's a trick that your brain plays on you!
Even if you have good eyesight, there's actually a hole in your vision,
called your blind spot. But your brain hides it from you!

The trick

First, try this test. Look straight at this picture of a cross, and a spot, with your nose pointing
at the space in between them. Close or cover your left eye, and with your right eye, focus on the cross.
Keep looking at the cross, and move your head slowly forward and backward.

At some point, the spot will disappear. It won't work if you look directly at the spot—
focus on the cross, so you are seeing the spot out of the corner of your eye.

What's going on?

At the back of each eyeball, you have a retina, a patch of light-detecting cells.
Each retina has a hole in it, where there's a bundle of nerves leading to your brain. But your brain
doesn't let you see this hole. You can only find it with a test like this one. When the spot disappears,
it's because it's lining up with the part of your eyeball that can't sense anything.

Why not try?

It gets even weirder. Try this test, which works in the exact same way. When the spot disappears, you don't see a gap—even though your eye can't actually detect anything there. Instead, you see the background pattern! Your brain has copied the background from around your blind spot, and used it to fill in the gap.

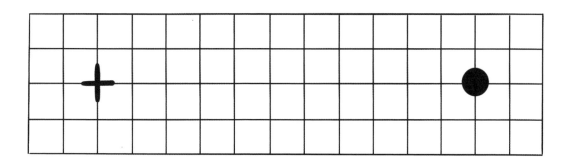

BLINK REFLEX

Imagine someone came up to you right now and threw some water in your face. The first thing you would do—before shouting "Hey!"—would be to screw your face up, and shut your eyes tightly. It's a reflex, or automatic movement, that your body does to protect you.

The trick

You'll need a clear plastic sheet, or you can use a door with a clear glass window if you have one.
Ask a friend to hold up the plastic in front of their face, or stand behind the window with their face up against it.

Now throw cotton wool balls, or small scrunched-up paper balls, at the glass or plastic, aiming at the person's eyes. What happens? Even though they know the balls can't hit their eyes, they will probably blink. In fact, even if you ask them to try not to blink, it's pretty hard to resist it!

What's going on?

We have reflexes so that we can act quickly for survival, without stopping to think. When we have a reflex reaction, the signals from our senses to our muscles shortcut the thinking part of our brain, so they happen without us having to make a decision—this makes the reaction faster and keeps us safe.

For example, blinking as soon as something comes near your eyes could save your eyesight. If you touch something very hot, you'll pull your hand away in a split second, so you don't get burned badly.

Did you know?

It is possible to stop reflex reaction, but you have to concentrate very hard to control your muscles with your thoughts instead. Can you do it with the blink reflex test?

THE ALIEN HAND

Tell a friend you're going to make them believe that a rubber glove is their own hand ... they'll think you're nuts!

The trick

Set up this trick carefully to make it work. First, you'll need a rubber glove. Fill it with rice or sand to make it more solid, and tie it with a rubber band. You'll also need two paintbrushes, a cloth (a dishtowel is ideal), and a tall, narrow box to act as a screen.

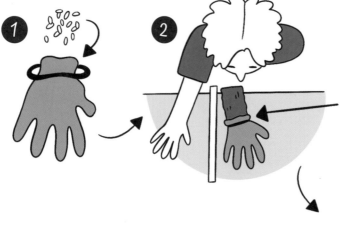

Your friend should sit at a table with the same hand that matches the glove (for example, their right hand) resting on the table, hidden from them behind the screen.

Place the rubber glove hand in front of them, next to the screen, where they can see it. Cover up the "wrist" of the fake hand with the cloth, as though it were a sleeve.

Now take your paintbrushes and brush the person's real hand and the rubber glove hand in exactly the same place and at the same time. Keep doing this, making sure the brushes do the exact same thing on both hands.

After a while, your friend should "feel" the brush on the rubber hand as if it were their own, and start to believe that the rubber hand really IS their hand!

118

What's going on?

This is another trick that shows we use more than one sense to decide what's happening—
and often, what you can see has a big effect on what you can feel. If you can see a hand in front
of you, being touched with a paintbrush, and you can feel the same sensation, your brain will assume the hand
it can see is your hand—even if it doesn't look realistic! This is sometimes called the "alien limb" illusion.

HOW MANY NOSES?

Your brain probably knows that you only have one nose—
but you can convince it you have two.

The trick

Cross your index and middle fingers over each other as far as you can, so that there's a gap between them, as shown below. Then, with one finger on each side of the tip of your nose, gently rub up and down. Told you—it feels like you've got two noses!

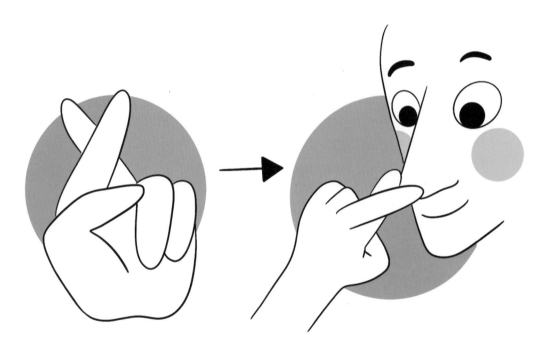

What's going on?

When your brain receives signals from your senses, it uses previous experiences to decide what's happening. In this trick, the outside edges of your fingers are both touching your nose. Normally, if the outside edges of your fingers both touch something at the same time, that means they are touching two different surfaces. So that's what your brain decides you can feel.

HOW LONG IS YOUR NOSE?

Not enough nose tricks for you? Here's another one!
This time, you need two people—not two noses!

the trick

This is called the "Pinocchio illusion." You and a friend sit in two chairs, one behind the other. The person at the back should put on a blindfold, then stroke their own nose, while reaching forward, and stroke or tap the other person's nose in exactly the same way. After a while, they'll start to feel like their nose is amazingly long!

What's going on?

In this trick, while you can't see anything, you are getting muddled messages from your sense of touch. One tells you that your own nose is being touched. The other tells you that you're touching the tip of a nose that is an arm's length away from your face. Your brain gets confused, and thinks your nose must be really long!

BIRD IN A CAGE

This simple toy, called a "thaumatrope," tricks your brain into combining two pictures into one.

the trick

Cut out a circle of white card or cardboard about 8 cm (3 inches) across. On one side, draw a bird. On the other side, the other way up, draw a cage. (Or any two pictures you want to combine, such as a fish and a bowl, or a horse and a rider.)

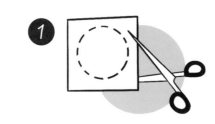

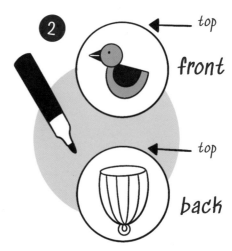

front

top

top

back

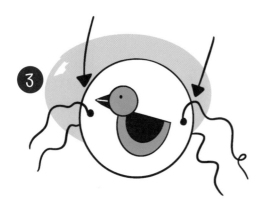

Make two holes at the sides of the card, and thread a loop of string through each hole. Hold the loops in your hands and flip the thaumatrope over and over until the strings are twisted, then pull them straight to make the thaumatrope spin.

What's going on?

When visual signals from your eyes are sent to your brain, they stay there for a split second. The thaumatrope fools your eyes by switching images even faster than this, which means you see the two separate images combined into one.

MOVIE-MAKING

You can use a similar effect to make a mini-movie!

the trick

You'll need a small, thick notepad, or a pad of sticky notes. On the outer edge, or corner, of the first page, draw a simple picture, like a stick person or a plant. On the next page, draw it again in the same place, but with a slight change of position. Change the picture on each page to show the person moving around, the plant growing flowers, or anything else you like. When you flip through the pad, you'll see a moving image!

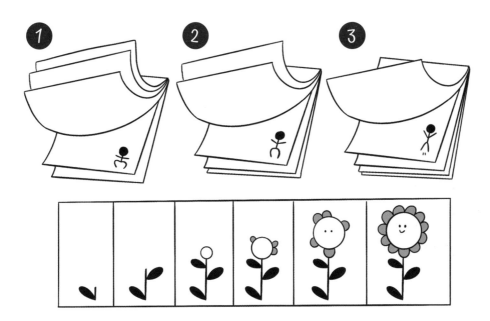

What's going on?

In everyday life, your brain is used to seeing things moving around.

When it sees a quick sequence of pictures, showing stages of something moving and changing, it pieces them together and "fills in" the gaps to see them as a moving object. Real movies work in the same way!

HOLE IN YOUR HAND

Make a hole right through your hand, with nothing more than a cardboard tube.
It's painless—that's a promise!

The trick

You'll need a cardboard tube that's about 30 cm (12 inches) long. With one hand, hold the tube up to one eye, and look through it, keeping both eyes open. Place your other hand next to the tube, about halfway along it, and look at your hand with your other eye. There it is—a hole in your hand!

What's going on?

Your two eyes send your brain two slightly different views of the world. Your brain combines them so you just see one image. When one eye is looking down the tube, and one is looking at your hand, your eyes are sending your brain two totally different images—but it still combines them!

THE FLYING SAUSAGE

To make a magical flying sausage, you just need your eyes, and your two index fingers.

The trick

Hold up your hands about 20-30 cm (8-12 inches) from your face, with your index fingers pointing at each other and almost touching, like this:

When you look straight at your fingers, you won't see anything odd. But stare through the gap, at the other side of the room, or the view though a window, and the sausage will appear, floating magically between your fingertips!

What's going on?

When you focus your eyes on something close to you, you see one clear image. But when you look into the distance, your eyes are focused on that, and they see your fingers in two different positions. The two images of your fingers overlap, and make a sausage out of your fingertips.

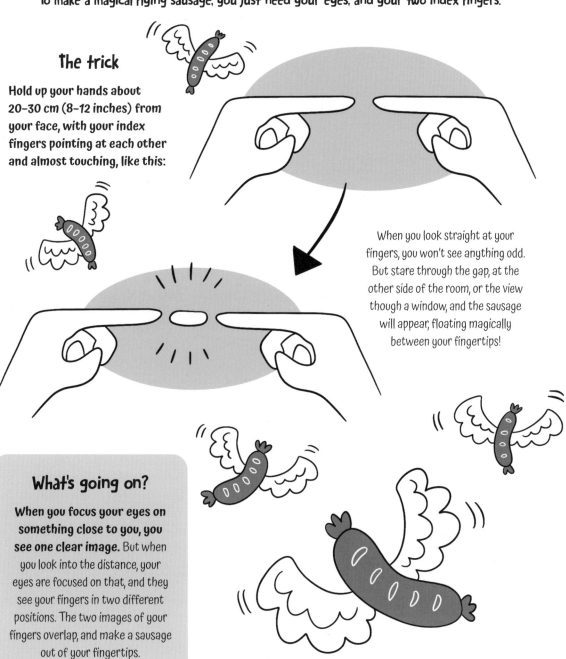

FLOATING ARMS

You can do this really simple trick in a doorway. You won't believe your arms!

the trick

Stand in a doorway (a small indoor one, not a huge one!). Keeping your arms straight, press the backs of your hands against the sides of the doorframe. Keep pressing as hard as you can, and stay in that position for one minute. When the minute is up, step out of the doorway, and relax your arms. They'll float upward, as if they were attached to helium balloons!

What's going on?

Your brain keeps sending the same signals to your arms to push outward, but they're stuck in the same position. After a while, your brain gets so used to doing this, it stops noticing what it's doing. When you relax, the signals still get sent for a while, but you don't feel as if they're coming from you. So your arms seem to float up by themselves!

GLOSSARY

After-image A reversed image that is left in your eye after you stop looking at something.

Air pressure The pushing force of the air in the atmosphere all around us.

Amber A hard material made from fossilized resin, a thick substance released by some types of trees.

Architect Someone who designs buildings.

Atmosphere The layer of air around the Earth.

Atoms The tiny units that materials are made of.

Attract To pull toward.

Blind spot A part of the retina, at the back of the eyeball, that cannot sense light.

Boiling point The temperature at which a substance boils, or changes from a liquid into a gas.

Camera obscura A dark room or box with a small hole to let in light, which creates an upside-down image opposite the hole.

Carbon An important element found in all living things.

Carbon dioxide A gas found in the air, and released when fuels burn.

Celsius A scale used for measuring temperature.

Center of gravity The part of an object around which an object's weight is evenly balanced.

Centripetal force The force that makes an object move in a circular path, by pulling it toward the middle of a circle.

Change of state A change in a substance between solid and liquid, or between liquid and gas.

Chemical reaction A change that happens when two or more substances combine and new, different substances are formed.

Chromatography Separating a substance out into its different ingredients by allowing it to spread through another material, such as paper.

Coandă effect The way liquid or gas appears to stick to a surface as it flows past.

Compass A magnetic device used to find north, and other directions.

Crystal A substance that naturally forms in regular geometric shapes.

Density How heavy something is for its size.

Electric charge A type of natural force, which can be positive or negative.

Electric shock A flow of electricity through the body, which can be harmful.

Electrons Tiny particles, which are usually part of atoms, but can also move as flow of electricity.

Elements Basic, pure materials that are made of only one type of atom. Oxygen, carbon, gold, and iron are examples of elements.

Energy The power to make things happen, move, or work.

Epsom salt A type of salt, similar to table salt, but made of a different combination of elements.

Expand To get bigger.

Fahrenheit A scale used for measuring temperature.

Fiber-optic cable A cable that carries information in the form of patterns of light.

Freezing point The temperature at which a liquid freezes, or turns into a solid.

Gramophone An old-fashioned machine for playing music.

GLOSSARY

Inertia The way an object keeps doing the same thing, either staying still or moving, until a force makes it change.

Levitate To hover in the air.

Light source Something from which light shines, such as a candle, a lightbulb, or the Sun.

Lodestone A kind of rock that is also a natural magnet.

Macaque A type of monkey.

Maglev A type of train that floats above the track using magnetic repulsion, instead of rolling on wheels.

Materials The various types of matter, or stuff, from which everything is made.

Molecules Tiny units made up of atoms, from which different substances are made.

Non-Newtonian fluid A liquid-like substance that becomes thicker or runnier in different situations.

Oobleck A type of non-Newtonian fluid made from cornstarch (cornflour) and water.

Oxygen A common gas that makes up part of the air, and that humans need to breathe.

Particles Tiny parts or bits.

Perspective The way the world looks from a particular angle, with farther-away objects appearing smaller.

Polymer A substance made of molecules that are made up of chains, or sequences of smaller molecules.

Proprioception The brain's sense of the position and the movement of the body.

Reflex An automatic body reaction that happens without you thinking about it.

Refraction The way light bends when it passes from one transparent substance, such as water, into another, such as air.

Repel To push away.

Repulsion Another word for repelling.

States of matter The states that a substance can exist in, such as solid, liquid, and gas.

Static electricity A type of electricity that does not flow, but builds up in an object.

Surface tension The way that molecules at the surface of water pull toward each other, making the water appear to have an invisible skin.

Triboluminescence A kind of light that glows from some materials when they are crushed or stretched.

Vibrate To shake quickly to and fro.

Viscosity The property of a liquid that describes how fast or slowly it will flow. Thicker liquids have a higher viscosity, and flow more slowly.